Trans/formations

Controversies in Contextual Theology Series

Trans/formations

Edited by

Lisa Isherwood

and

Marcella Althaus-Reid

scm press

British Library Cataloguing in Publication data

A catalogue record for this book is available
from the British Library

978 0 334 04343 0

First published in 2009 by SCM Press
13–17 Long Lane,
London EC1A 9PN

www.scm-canterburypress.co.uk

SCM Press is a division of
SCM-Canterbury Press Ltd

Typeset by Regent Typesetting
Printed and bound in Great Britain by
CPI Antony Rowe, Chippenham SN14 6LH

Contents

List of Contributors

Marcella Althaus-Reid was Professor of Contextual Theology at the University of Edinburgh. She died in 2009.

Hannah Buchanan is a 28-year-old woman who made the decision to do something about lifelong feelings of gender dysphoria. She holds a degree in English and Sociology.

Krzysztof Bujnowski is a transman and a supporter of feminism; and his academic interests are in the sociology and politics of difference. He co-chairs the South West Transgender Equality Network and Western Boys (which is a support group for transmen and not a mythopoetic refuge for disaffected wranglers).

Marie Cartier is affiliated to Claremont Graduate University and has published in the areas of sexuality and gender as well as creating exhibitions related to female sexuality.

John Clifford is Professor of Theatre and Bill Findlay Fellow of Stage Translation at Queen Margaret University College, Edinburgh, and Associate Playwright of the Playwrights' Studio, Scotland.

Susannah Cornwall is Research Fellow at the University of Exeter and has published extensively on intersex, embodiment and theologies of sexuality.

Malcolm Himschoot is a transman, minister of the MCC in the USA and an independent scholar working on issues of inclusion.

B. K. Hipsher is an MCC minister living in Canada and is a PhD student at the University of Winchester working on the history of feminist theology.

Lisa Isherwood is Professor of Feminist Liberation Theologies and Director of Theological Partnerships at the University of Winchester.

Virginia Ramey Mollenkott is Professor Emeritus at the William Paterson University of New Jersey and the author or co-author of 13 books, including *Omnigender* and *Transgender Journeys*.

Lewis Reay is a transman, member of MCC in Edinburgh and an independent scholar working in the area of gender.

Liz Stuart is Professor of Christian Theology and Pro Vice Chancellor of the University of Winchester. She is the author of many books in the area of sexuality and gender, and executive editor of the international journal *Theology & Sexuality*.

Siân Taylder is a transwoman and PhD student at the University of Winchester working in the area of sexuality and gender.

Introduction

LISA ISHERWOOD

It is at the crossroads that Wisdom takes her stand. (Prov. 8.2)

The desire to edit a book on Trans-theology arose from concern and at times outrage at the narrow and ever-narrowing boundaries of traditional theological thinking. We know that the debate still rages over gay and lesbian inclusion in churches and the rights and wrongs of lesbian and gay lifestyles. Some thought, well at least a pamphlet or two, has been given to transsexuals and the churches, but the issue is highly contentious and silence is usually the deafening response. As ever, most churches are mystified by the notion of gender and so the debate in transgender issues is one that they have as yet to be persuaded they need, let alone that they should, theologically engage in a serious way.

In contrast, we are mystified that they do not embrace the debates and indeed lead the way in radical thinking fuelled by the transgendered and transsexual members of their churches. After all there is a very 'trans' core to this incarnational religion that they declare to be the redemptive reality of the world. Why, we wonder, would such a destabilizing religion lend itself to stabilizing categories such as gender and sex, categories which in their fixed and stable form underpin so many of the world's most abusive institutions from marriage to genocidal capitalism. A mystery indeed!

How can we claim that Christianity is destabilizing? We realize that this in itself is contentious, but we believe that we have good grounds to suggest it and that the argument rests on the declaration that the all-powerful creator of the universe left the heavens and became a baby, not one with superhuman powers but rather a very vulnerable child born to people living under political oppression. As if this transformation were not enough, we are told stories of further radical transformations in the life of this man Jesus of Nazareth, all of which are part of our redemptive history. From man to risen friend who even travelled to the depth of hell to become the risen assurance of transformed life and to ascend as companion in the struggle and from there to the altars of much of the Christian world as the real presence in bread and wine, transformations across a wide range of material substances and through various manifestations, all of which proclaim for the believer the nature of God and the ways in which salvation occurs. The author of John's Gospel tells us that God pitched a tent among us, that is to say a very flexible structure, one that moves with the winds of change, one that is mobile, one that can be pitched in many different locations and one that is permeable yet firm. There are absolutely no fixed boundaries in this performance of salvation history among us but rather an ongoing performance of flexible boundaries which successive generations of believers have tried to fix for their own security. Of course, as Bob Goss reminds us, Christianity does not offer security or even survival: there is no survivability ethic at its heart but rather disruptions to fixed-and-known cherished ways (Goss 2002).

Even if this were acknowledged by traditional theology there are those in church circles who we are sure would wish to claim that issues such as transgender and transsexual lifestyles are a new craze no doubt to do with a more liberal society. This would be a very selective and 'straight' reading of our history, however, which does not bear real scrutiny.

As early as 1902, Ernst von Dobschuetz was surmising that the Apocryphal Acts were written in the genre of the Hellenistic romantic novel as Christians thought this would be a good way to spread the word in an underhand way (Burrus 1987, p. 11). Kerenyi traces the genre back to the first century BC and to Seneca (Burrus 1987, p. 16). He sees cultic roots in the stories since the women in these stories have very passionate sex with a god, are then threatened but saved. In the story of Io we see that once saved she is referred to as a virgin who shunned the love of men. Kerenyi suggests that this motif transfers itself very easily to the Christian stories, making them legends and not novels. There is a very strong body of scholarship (MacDonald 1983) which suggests that they are folktales and as such they claim to present history. Folktales serve two opposing purposes: they stabilize society and at the same time they destabilize society. They can define the identity of those who are dissatisfied with society and become a source of strength for that group.

What we find in many of the stories are women who defy physical boundaries and so question social sexual roles by their actions. These days they may be called queer narratives. The women are always the heroines, even when an apostle like Paul is part of the story, because they are faithful and true and overcome adversity and threats to themselves. Thecla is an interesting character: to our modern eyes and ways of understanding is she a transvestite? Is she transgendered? Or is she transsexual? Or is this motif used to tell us something of significance about the relationship of people who become Christian with their environment? Contemporary scholarship is no longer content to leave the argument that she and others cross-dressed for the sake of safety. After all, in Thecla's story, she does not cross-dress from the beginning even though she is travelling and at some risk, she only cross-dresses after baptism. And of course, this is in strict contravention of scriptural command (Deut. 22.5). Transvestites were quite common in some pagan cults where they were associated with Aphrodite of Cyprus: however, this does not help explain Thecla. The clue to Thecla may be found when she is thrown to the beasts but not killed: the tale relays that she found herself clothed by God. John Anson suggests that this is perhaps a literal fulfilment of the putting on of Christ that Paul speaks about in baptism and so for him the donning of men's clothes is simply another step in this process that started in the arena with the beasts (Anson 1974). He continues that a faith based on Galatians 3.27–8 would mean followers would embody a state of primal perfection that overcame all distinctions, including that of sex. In putting on Christ, followers would attempt to appropriate his male form (Anson 1974, p. 7). There is of course a real danger here that we see perfect creation as male and so women have to disappear, or at least cross-dress in order to be saved! The *Gospel of Thomas* may be seen as the transgendered or even transsexual gospel where it reads 'For every woman who makes herself a male will enter the Kingdom of heaven' (*Gosp. Thom.* 114). This was made quite explicit in some baptismal rites, such as those among the

Valentinians where bisexual fusion was enacted and women were transformed into males.

Another possible background for Thecla's actions may have been rooted in Montanism where the women prophets Prisca and Maximilla had prominent roles. They had many visions and understood themselves as female Christs. This understanding was based on their reading of Galatians 3.27–8 whereby once the distinctions and divisions were overcome they were free to embrace their divine natures. There are many such stories and indeed they are found in many of the religions of the time as well as ancient mythologies. While we want to reject the idea that this has to be understood as the donning of male perfection, we also want to question that it was purely a device to protect chastity. Even though many of these women donned men's clothes after they ran away from marriages or engagements and wandered in the world, there is much more to this than meets the eye. We wish to argue that they understood their male attire as connected in overcoming the binary opposites of gender that set in place unequal lived reality. Cross-dressing implies a starting point and a place towards which one is aiming and so serves to highlight gender polarity since clothes allow us to play with identity and they aid that becoming a physical embodied performance. Cross-dressing creates an illusion for the user and the observer or, as van Gennep puts it, it is a liminal space allowing movement across boundaries and transversing margins which confine (Suthrell 2004, p. 18). Cross-dressing is an ingenious tool as it does not fit categories of sex or gender alone and as such exposes both and so in this way is a form of gender iconography, making visible the spaces of possibility which are closed off by dichotomous conceptualization.

Ritual cross-dressing, which predated Christian cross-dressing, has at its heart the notion of returning to wholeness, believing that it allows a very deep experience of gender, both one's own and the other. In some societies cross-dressing represents magical qualities that are signalled by its ambiguity. So Christian cross-dressing has a cultural heritage and, in taking seriously the message of equality of the Christian gospel, those who did it queered gender in order to find a way of living that radical equality. After all, once we engage in confusing the categories it leads to their breakdown as oppositional points of reference, and we need to ensure that we do not replace them with points along an old axis. We are perhaps beginning to understand what our cross-dressed fore-sisters were doing and can begin to ask if we should be doing it too.

It seems entirely possible that these stories of gender-bending were written by and for women who wished to subvert the social order. Possibly they represented wishes rather than realities at the time that they were written but it may also be the case that they traced back to the time of Jesus and had a kernel of truth embedded in the lives of women around him. Women who break out from the norm in any age face the threat of physical violence and I find it extremely fascinating that their way of remaining safe was to keep transgressing the norm (Isherwood 2000). Indeed, later male readers often praise them for escaping their feminine natures. John Chrysostom was ecstatic that Olympius may be said to be male, having risen above her female nature. Women like Thecla both cut their hair and wore male clothing, which is an extremely transgressive action in the world in which she is portrayed. These women were not all transsexual but they pushed the gender boundaries very hard in order to create space in which to flourish. Their stories are inspirational in that they provide a memory that is counter to the 'good-girl' image that we have been presented with by the church hierarchy. They ask questions about engendered spaces that are as relevant today as they were then and they show that storytelling and action can be subversive. They tell a different story and so make possible a different reality.

Richard Rambuss has undertaken some interesting research in the area of erotic desire and the sacred within Christian history and what he has uncovered is the way in which the sacred erotic transgresses the boundaries of vanilla heterosexuality, that form of sexuality that is paradoxically upheld with such vigour by Christian morality (Rambuss 1998). There are similarities between his work and that of Bataille who signalled that the transgressive is at the heart of the erotic in its full and religious state. This is summed up by Michael Warner who says 'religion makes available a language of ecstasy, a horizon of significance within which transgressions against the normal order of the world and the boundaries of self can be seen as good things' (Warner in Rambuss 1998, p. 58).

Rambuss takes us on a magical and at times mind-bending tour of religious devotion where the iconized body of Christ is the desirable object, the body that is not there for reproduction but is nonetheless lusted after and penetrated. This body becomes fully eroticized through the desire that those worshipping it direct towards it and receive from it. What is interesting for the present work is that this iconized body of Christ is very changeable and does not in any way at all hold fast to or fix sex, gender or sexuality either in itself or in those who adore it. Catherine of Sienna marries Christ who crosses genders for Catherine who eventually becomes engaged passionately with, sinking into the flesh of, a female Christ. Catherine is but one example of many littered throughout Christian history who engaged with the body of Christ only to experience a crossing of gender either for Christ or for themselves. Many writings and art works show the body of Christ as very fluid, at times even appearing as physically female.

The erotic desiring of Christ and its trans-consequences is not restricted to Catholic Christians, and in the writings of Quakers such as the missionary couple Katherine Evans and Sarah Cheevers we see a very interesting phenomenon. For Katherine and Sarah, both married women with children, Christ was the one who kindled and sanctified their love for each other: 'the Lord has joined us together and wo be to them that should part us' (Rambuss 1998, p. 94). What we read is their revisioning of their gender expectations and their erotic connections – this is not to simply state a rather unremarkable binary move from heterosexual to homosexual: their stories are more complex and show how 'within Christ' many boundaries are blurred and categories do not work as well as society may hope they would. In this mix of religion and the erotic, devotion becomes heightened and, as we see, all the normal boundaries become incidental and of no importance at all.

No look at boundary crossing and flexible edges in Christian history would be complete without a look at Margery Kempe who places before us the embodiment of moving beyond otherness and who more than most illuminates Heyward's assertion that 'our sensuality is the foundation of our authority' (Heyward 1989, p. 93).

Margery, like Catherine, weds God but this is still the Godhead who for her is father, son and spirit, who we should understand as female, with a very important addition – Margery herself. We are boldly told that God himself declared to her 'and God is in you and you are in him' (Kempe 1985, p. 124). This is a very extraordinary marriage, one that crosses all kinds of boundaries and opens up all kinds of possibilities. Everything is thrown into disarray and what emerges is a relationality based on radical subjectivity through which Margery's self becomes bigger. Her vision of being wedded to and an integral part of the Godhead enables her to experience her edges as expanded, but at the same time she moves around her own core in a dance of autoerotic/erotic self-discovery. The nomad in her experiencing Margery the father, Margery the son, Margery the spirit at the same time as embracing father, son and spirit [female] as wedded lover. Of course, in this mutual subjectivity father, son and spirit all experience their divinity through Margery. Subjectivity is heightened the more identity becomes nomadic but this is no mere gender performance – father, son and spirit are all interchangeable and as such go beyond gender categories and into animal, mineral, ether, bread, wine, presence and absence and so much more. This is a subjectivity with no edges, a contradiction, a boundarylessness that gives meaning but fixes nothing. Margery is released into a fuller life through changing 'the subject' and she expands the boundaries of theology by being so liberated. She propels us to explore limitless embodiment and radical subjectivity and in so doing to truly incarnate the gospel of radical equality. Reflecting on her life we may begin to speculate that while we continue to allow the enactment of fixed binary opposites, stable and unequal categories on our bodies through sexual stereotyping or sexual intimacy we fail to open to the diverse/surprising wonder of radical incarnation.

We see then that far from having no Christian history which offers starting points for theological reflection on trans-bodies and lives we in fact have quite a wealth right at the heart of things, from cross-dressing saints to Margery who seems to defy all categories but may be called a transtheoerotic in that she changed her gender relationships quite regularly with the Godhead who itself underwent subtle changes in her theological hands. It may be true to say that it is only with our modern take on what sex and gender might be that we have managed to fix what was quite unfixed for our Christian forebears who after all followed a religion that declared in Christ there was no male or female. Feminist theologians have concentrated on what the economic and social aspects of this statement might be, understanding it to challenge the way in which the world is set out divided among sexes (Isherwood 2006), but perhaps the time has come to take that reflection further and ask what it says to each Christian in their embodied lived reality.

The articles in this book are reflective and experiential as well as academically and theologically courageous and creative. They bring to light a range of experience and challenge through their honesty. There are voices and views expressed here that should never have been silenced or ignored, because theology is all the richer for engaging with them.

Susannah Cornwall demonstrates how medical and social essentialist models lead to stigmatizing of individuals and further how the medical model is driven by a desire to make people 'normal'. This is a trend she deeply regrets and she further calls to task even queer theory itself which she feels does not always allow for diversity beyond already stabilized categories. Sexual identity, she tells us, is not the only way to differentiate from heteronormativity. Reflecting on apopahtic theology, she suggests that as God is never fully known then becoming like God may involve giving up what we think we have known about ourselves as human – this is a positive unknowing rather than a passive ignorance.

Hannah Buchanan takes us on a deeply personal reflection and in this moving piece attests to the power of the grace of God to work in all creation and beyond the limits of a narrow and ever-narrowing Christian theology put forward by the churches.

Virginia Mollenkott invites the churches to recognize and accept the gifts that transpeople bring to their congregations. She argues very powerfully that the Bible is transgender friendly, that transfolk help congregations face up to and overcome the limitations of gender stereotyping. Further the presence of transpeople is a constant reminder of the diverse glory of God's creation. She reminds us that until recently transpeople were viewed as gifted bridge-builders within certain communities and thus welcomed for those skills. In addition, because of life experience, many transpeople are specialists in sex, gender and sexuality, areas that she feels the churches need much help in addressing. Perhaps one of the biggest strengths Mollenkott identifies is the position of ambiguity which she believes challenges the churches' addiction to certainty.

Krzysztof Bujnowski takes us on a journey of an ordinary bloke living in an extraordinary body which made him a refugee in his own country, a stranger in a strange land. This piece takes us on a journey which the author tells us is as important as arriving and it spells out very clearly the power of gender in society, a society that can make even posting a letter an exhausting task for those who have to be on guard about gender performance. What we feel here is the complexities of body–mind conjunctions and the complete inability of Church doctrine to begin to understand this particular lived experience.

Siân Taylder, who like Krzy is also from a Catholic background, introduces us to the theology of a woman who is not quite what she seems. There is much anger in this article about the way in which people are dismissed under trite clichés, secular and theological, and there is also much pleasure in understanding the revolutionary potential of an angry transsexual with an axe to grind. That axe falls squarely on the Catholic Church and its appeal to natural moral law when considering the question of transsexuality, and it takes apart the complementary assumptions held by the Church as well as the reproductive imperative which lurks behind ideas of sexuality and gender.

B. K. Hipsher argues that transgender covers a wide range of persons some of whom are more troubling to churches than others but all of which should be seen as part of the rich diversity and ever-changing nature of the divine. It is because a transgender image of God is so unsettling to people that we are compelled to argue for it because it moves us beyond all we think we know about God and about humanity. It gives fullness to the idea of ongoing incarnation.

Marie Cartier asks us to focus on a very familiar figure in a very unfamiliar way by describing to us the butch inside James Dean. She argues that in his film *Rebel without a Cause* he was asking the question why does gender have to be played in a certain way? Further, that this performance based on that of a butch woman of the 1950s laid some foundations for what we now call queer nation. In the new man identity that

Dean was forming it is possible to detect traces of butch/femme relationships and therefore a questioning of what gender is about and what it may be.

Elizabeth Stuart contends that the Eucharist erases sex altogether, indeed that the Eucharist is itself transsexual as it takes sex into the realm of the symbolic and offers many displacements. Through its celebration we are able to move more easily to a new identity, one that is unstable and non-sexed. Stuart argues that transsexual people must be welcomed and honoured in church circles but must also take up the Eucharist challenge of erasure. In other words, they must not take comfort in a new identity but must realize that it too is unstable and has no ultimate meaning: they must live it through resisting gender scripts rather than reaffirming them.

Malcolm Himschoot offers another type of liturgy from that offered by Stuart: his reflections begin in anger as well as in the belief that transgendered people offer a rich theological dimension in the areas of embodiment and relationality as well as reflections on the ongoing creation of God. Anger seems an appropriate starting point for this liturgical reflection since anger springs from hope that things may be different and needs to be accompanied by courage if it is indeed to make things different.

Lewis Reay wishes to queer the eunuchs and does so by taking us on a fascinating rereading of some biblical texts that will be familiar to many and of some doctrinal understandings. Reay points out that the earth creature *adam* was not male or female but full of the potentiality that is possible in God and this included gender potential. Trans- and intersexed people then mirror the very complexities of this original earth creature in their own imaging of the divine. Further, they can present a challenge to all to move away from the binary oppositions of gender that had no part in the original blessing of God's creation. Transgender theology is inclusive as it inhabits the luminal space which is God's territory.

And finally, in a different key, John Clifford asks us to consider God's New Frock – enjoy the spectacle!

In these chapters you will experience slightly differing views and many different lived experiences and each one asks you the question of sex and gender. How much pressure is on you to be just the right mix of all the right qualities according to your genitals, and in the end do your genitals make you the person you are? Despite more liberal attitudes in some quarters it still appears to be the case that if boys will be girls they had better be ladies (Namaste 2000, p. 24). The old schemes of gender still lurk within even our most liberal thinking and are certainly present in our medical and psychological assessments. This is graphically illustrated in the story of Drusilla (Beard 2008) who is representative of many others in her position. For her first interview with doctors regarding transition she was found not to be serious enough about wanting to be a woman because she attended the interview in trousers. We have a long way to go in relation to unpacking and celebrating trans-reality and even further to go in creating theology that is inclusive and challenged by the variety and glory of diverse gender. The visibility of transpeople has increased considerably since the 1990s, according to Susan Stryker, and has rapidly moved through a series of medical and psychological models, having been still considered as homosexuality as recently as 1973. It is encouraging to us as theologians that our history has not been able to erase transpeople totally and that redemption history may be read as best lived in that trans/luminal embodied space.

Marcella and I talked about this book for some time and then began to ask people to contribute and it was at this time that Marcella became ill. Despite this, she was able to keep her interest in the project and she did manage to read several of the papers. It was a great joy to her to know that SCM Press would publish the book as she felt many others may not have had the courage or foresight, so for this we are both grateful to Natalie Watson.

It was my great honour to work with Marcella and to call her my friend and I am indebted because her integrity gave me the courage to ask the hard questions, her sharp intellect challenged and made me go further and her wit and sense of fun brought out the naughty girls in us both!!! Before she died, she made me promise that I would speak of us as a theological team, working from intellectual and deeply affectionate closeness, working from the heart and the head and engaging in the abundant joy and laughter of the *caminata* we shared.

Go well my friend, un abrazo.

References

Anson, John (1974), 'The Female Transvestite in Early Monasticism: The Origin and Development of a Motif'. *Berkeley, Viator* 5, pp. 1–32.

Beard, Richard (2008), *Becoming Drusilla: One Life, Two Friends, Three Genders* (London: Random House).

Burrus, Virginia (1987), *Chastity as Autonomy: Women in the Stories of the Apocryphal Acts* (Lewiston: Edwin Mellen Press).

Goss, Robert (2002), *Queering Christ: Beyond Jesus Acted Up* (Cleveland: Pilgrim Press).

Heyward, Carter (1989), *Touching Our Strength: The Erotic as Power and the Love of God* (San Francisco: Harper Collins).

Isherwood, Lisa, ed. (2000), *The Good News of the Body: Sexual Theology & Feminism* (Sheffield: Sheffield Academic Press).

Isherwood, Lisa (2006), *The Power of Erotic Celibacy* (London: T&T Clark).

Kempe, Margery (1985), *The Book of Margery Kempe* (London: Penguin).

MacDonald, Dennis (1983), *The Legend and the Apostles: The Battle for Paul in Story and Canon* (Philadelphia: Westminster Press).

Namaste, Vivane (2000), *Invisible Lives: The Erasure of Transsexual and Transgendered People* (Chicago: The University of Chicago Press).

Rambuss, Richard (1998), *Closet Devotions* (Durham, NC: Duke University Press).

Suthrell, Charlotte (2004), *Unzipping Gender, Sex, Cross-Dressing and Culture* (Oxford: Berg).

1

Apophasis and Ambiguity: The 'Unknowingness' of Transgender

SUSANNAH CORNWALL

Introduction

> The medical approach to gender variance, and the creation of transsexuality, has resulted in a governance of trans bodies that restricts our ability to make gender transitions which do not yield membership in a normative gender role. The self-determination of trans people in crafting our gender expression is compromised by the rigidity of the diagnostic and treatment criteria. (Spade 2006, p. 329)

Transgendered lawyer and activist Dean Spade's line of argument is a far from uncommon one, though no less persuasive for that. According to Spade, medical and surgical standards for the treatment of gender variance work to eradicate liminality and to erase, through careful crafting, bodies and identities deemed to question or subvert the social norms whereby sexes, genders and sexualities must all map onto each other unproblematically. Spade claims that trans patients who actively *want* to have genitals which appear ambiguous or atypical – for instance, female-to-male transsexuals who undergo phallic augmentation but who also choose not to have their vaginal opening closed up – are unlikely to find sympathetic surgeons, since 'doctors . . . only seek to produce genitals that fit into one of two narrowly defined options' (Spade 2006, pp. 323–4). It is important to note that such a narrative seems to be ratified by stories from intersex too, suggesting that socio-medical discomfort at unusual genitalia is aroused not solely by people who have chosen intervention to render them so but also by individuals in whom unusual genitalia have 'naturally' (that is, spontaneously) occurred. Howard Devore, a clinical psychotherapist who has worked extensively with intersexed children and their families and is opposed to early genital surgery after being treated for extreme hypospadias[1] in 18 operations throughout his own childhood, says,

> The doctors insist that you can't let a child go to school with ambiguous genitals, but the genitals they created were certainly strange-looking . . . There was no reason for some of the work that they did on me outside of arrogance or incompetence . . . If they had just left my urinary meatus . . . where it was, at the base of my penis right by the scrotum, I could have avoided at least 12 of those surgeries. (Devore 1999, pp. 80–1)

Devore identifies medical arrogance, rather than altruism, as a possible reason for the surgeons' attempts to 'perfect' his own 'imperfect' genital region – a desire to show just what modern surgery can do. Others have suggested that it is for specifically heteronormative reasons that ambiguous genitals are so often 'disappeared' in the case of intersex, or not allowed to be created in the case of trans-surgery; in this account, within a heteronormative paradigm, it is necessary that 'ambiguous' genitals are made unambiguous, made to tell the 'truth' of a person's status, as 'normal' unambiguous genitals supposedly manage to do unproblematically.

Anyone who has ever questioned the biological essentialism innate in the notion that 'vagina' always and without exception means 'girl', and that 'girl' always and without exception means 'sexually attracted to and/or active with males' will recognize that the situation is far more complicated than that. Such essentialist assumptions have contributed

---

1 Hypospadias is a condition where the urinary opening appears somewhere along the underside of the penis rather than at its tip. Hypospadias is not exclusively a result of intersex conditions, and sometimes occurs in non-intersexed males, but can also be part of an intersexed genital presentation as in Devore's own case.

to a secretive, stigmatizing medical model and early surgery paradigm for intersex – and one which has not yet been entirely left behind – is hugely problematic.[2] However, although the colonization of atypical bodies and genital configurations is ethically pressing, and continues to prompt important work across medical and social-scientific discourse, here I focus on a slightly different issue. Crucially, and just as problematically, it is not only heteronormative surgeons who have been accused of desiring conceptual control over the body stories disseminated by people who have atypical configurations of genitals and gender either by birth or by election. Transgendered scholar and artist Susan Stryker remarks,

> Queer studies, though putatively antiheteronormative, sometimes fails to acknowledge that same-sex object choice is not the only way to differ from heterosexist cultural norms, that transgender phenomena can also be antiheteronormative, or that transgender phenomena constitute an axis of difference that cannot be subsumed to an object-choice model of antiheteronormativity. As a result, queer studies sometimes perpetuates what might be called 'homonormativity', that is, a privileging of homosexual ways of differing from heterosexual norms, and an antipathy (or at least an unthinking blindness) toward other modes of queer difference. (Stryker 2006, p. 7)

In short, claims Stryker, although transgender studies arose in the context of existing academic feminist and queer work (Stryker 2006, p. 7), and while queer studies 'remains the most hospitable place to undertake transgender work' (Stryker 2004, p. 213), 'queer' is too frequently

---

2 Alice Dreger, a historian and activist for intersex, comments that much heterosexist significance is invested in the genitals, and particularly the penis, even in the surgeries performed on very young intersexed children. Dreger says, 'Much is expected of penises by intersexuality doctors, especially by pediatric urologists. In order for a penis to count as acceptable – "functional" – it must be or have the potential to be big enough to be recognized as a "real" penis . . . Intersex surgeons make their decisions and incisions within a heterosexist framework . . . Consequently, while much is demanded of a newborn's penis, very little is needed for a surgically constructed vagina to count as "functional" . . . It basically has to be a hole big enough to fit a typical-sized penis' (Dreger 1998, pp. 183–4).

still used as shorthand for gay or lesbian; and 'all too often transgender phenomena are misapprehended through a lens that privileges sexual orientation and sexual identity as the primary means of differing from heteronormativity' (Stryker 2004, pp. 213–14).[3] That the very binary homosexual/heterosexual cannot stand is exemplified in those who are biologically 'homosexual' but socially 'heterosexual', which includes many transgendered people. However, as Stryker notes, there are some who reject socially 'heterosexual' transgender as a valid form of identity expression for those who would query the validity of the heterosexual matrix. In this account, 'straight' transgendered people are simply not queer enough.

Trans(gendered) trans(ition) and apophasis

In this chapter, I contend that a rejection of proscriptive homonormativity, an acknowledgement that it is no more inherently liberating or anti-binary than heteronormativity, may find resonance with the tradition of apophatic or negative theology. This, I suggest, means there is a precedent for exploring the uncertainty, liminality and even paradox of human identity (and in this case, sex-gender identity) from within the theological tradition – even if such 'fuzziness' has fallen from favour in much recent mainstream theology. Importantly, given Stryker's assertion that homonormativity is not an adequate successor to heteronormativity, classic apophatic theologies stress that rejecting a given image or metaphor for God as too limiting or simplistic must not then entail the unproblematic adoption of an 'opposite' image. I argue that apophatically influenced theologies, those which resist a finality of understanding and are grounded instead in a proactive *unknowing* about God, might,

3 Stryker believes that this happens because queer politics and studies 'remain invested . . . in an underlying conceptual framework that is problematized by transgender phenomena' (Stryker 2006, p. 7). This, she says, arises from an overemphasis on the *sex* of the 'sexual object', the primary thing that differentiates homosexual ('queer') from heterosexual eroticism (Stryker 2006, p. 7) but which itself begins to be disrupted by those whose sex and gender may not cohere in expected ways.

in fact, be important sites of solidarity for transgender. In this way, transgender need not be unproblematically aligned with either heteronormative or homonormative modes of discourse, but might stand in tension with both, inherently neither fully like nor fully unlike either. It might, as Sarah Coakley comments on Gregory of Nyssa's gender theory (discussed later in this chapter), be a means of wending a *transformative* way through the binaries (see Coakley 2000, p. 67).

I also hold that, despite Stryker's misgivings about queer as an overarching discourse, specifically queer *theologies* have already begun to move beyond a uniquely homosexual positionality and resistance to heterosexual norms, and hold within themselves the legacy of the apophasis which has not always been valued within mainstream theology. As Stryker herself argues, there are 'other modes of queer difference' (Stryker 2006, p. 7) than homonormative ones. In fact, to follow David M. Halperin, queer is

> by definition, *whatever* is at odds with the normal, the legitimate, the dominant. *There is nothing in particular to which it necessarily refers* . . . 'Queer' . . . demarcates not a positivity but a positionality vis-à-vis the normative – a positionality that is not restricted to lesbians and gay men. (Halperin 1995, p. 62)

Queer theologies in particular, as opposed to broader queer theories, have the potential to stand over against constricting, limiting ideologies because, as Gerard Loughlin comments, 'theology relativizes all earthly projects, insisting that to understand ourselves we must first understand our orientation to the unknown from which all things come and to which they return' (Loughlin 2007a, p. 7). Queer theologies emphasize the profoundly ineffable and indescribable nature of the manner in which human sex, gender and sexuality fit together, just as negative theologies have emphasized the unknowability of God. I examine this in more detail below.

I conclude that, since theology points to a God who is not fully known, part of becoming like that God is being prepared to give up part of what we believe we know about ourselves as humans. This, I argue, may include gendered identity. This applies partly but not uniquely in the case of transgender; it is those who do *not* have 'unusual' configurations of sex and gender who must prophetically cede their privilege first, as I argue below. Truly apophatic theology should open up the possibility for a broad, creative picture of God, rejecting the limitedness of metaphors rooted in finite human conception. Similarly, it must be acknowledged that those who choose gender transition (with or without surgery) are *not* necessarily unproblematically reinforcing heterosexual norms, even if they are not questioning them in exactly the way that some non-trans, homosexual-identified people may prefer.

'Nothing to Hold on to': Truth beyond Knowing

Apophasis was an important element in the thought of early Christian theologians including Clement of Alexandria, Basil of Caesarea, Gregory of Nyssa and John Chrysostom, and (later) Pseudo-Dionysius and Aquinas. It emphasized journeying, movement and change, rather than apotheosizing fixity and stasis. Apophatic expressions in the historic theologians sometimes take the form of systematic progressions through a series of denials that particular qualities are truly applicable to God. For example, Janet P. Williams summarizes of Pseudo-Dionysius,

> In the last chapter [of Dionysius' *Mystical Theology*], the great affirmations of Christian faith are dealt with – God is Life, Light, Love, Goodness, Wisdom, Power, and so on – and these too are all denied: they are not true. This rejection of all the precious truths of Scripture is . . . met at the very last by the terse statement that God, the 'supreme Cause', is 'free of every limitation, beyond every limitation; it is also beyond every denial.' Here we have simply, as Dionysius says, run out of words: the soul has nothing left, nothing to hold on to. (Williams 2004, pp. 190–1).

Unlike kataphatic or affirmative theology which 'proceeds from the first and few affirmations nearest God's own ineffable simplicity down to the last and many assertions of variegated symbols for the deity' (Rorem 1984, p. 88), the denials or negations 'begin with these last few things and become fewer and less verbal as they ascend toward the speechless' (Rorem 1984, p. 88). Importantly, though, notes Paul Rorem of the *Mystical Theology*, the patterns of affirmation and negation are not 'random' but are sited firmly in Pseudo-Dionysius' broad project of interpreting Scripture (Rorem 1984, pp. 88, 89): Dionysius wants to encourage his audience to be similarly sceptical of superficial or 'surface' meanings when reading the Scriptures, instead rejecting them in favour of deeper meanings (Rorem 1984, p. 94). Here kataphasis and apophasis work in tandem: affirmation and negation are *both* useful in trying to spiral upward toward God; but 'the conceptions gained in this process of biblical hermeneutics will themselves be negated eventually, not in yet another interpretation but in an abandonment entirely in the silent approach to that which is ultimately transcendent' (Rorem 1984, p. 89).[4]

Pseudo-Dionysius and other early figures were extremely influential on Aquinas' expression of negative theology, in which the reason that no claim about what God is positively like can be made is fundamentally because God does not exist in the same way that other things exist. God is indescribable, because human metaphor always falls short of communicating perfection. God also cannot be described by God's effects, because even cumulatively these cannot add up to a full knowledge of what God is. Aquinas patterns a Dionysian structure of 'procession and return', though, like Pseudo-Dionysius himself he avoids 'the simple isolation of negative theology, preferring to note its inter-dependence with affirmative theology as a unified method' (Rorem 1984, p. 148). For

4 Rorem concludes that, for Pseudo-Dionysius at least, the purpose of negation is to strip away falsehood so that truer knowledge of God is ultimately made possible (Rorem 1984, p. 96). It thus seems eventually to be subsumed to a more conventional project of *kataphasis*, unlike in its later use as taken up by, for example, Meister Eckhart, Henry Suso, and the author of *The Cloud of Unknowing* (see Rorem 1984, pp. 143–4). Even if Rorem is correct that Dionysius' aim is eventual *knowing* rather than perpetual *un*knowing, however, it is still possible to identify in Dionysius a tension around what it is and is not possible to 'know' in the first place.

Aquinas, there *is* an actual reality in and of God – it is just, comments Fran O'Rourke, that human language and understanding can never allow us to access it (O'Rourke 1992, pp. 47–8, 56).[5] The soul can, however, become 'united with God in the manner which is possible in this life, i.e. when it knows him to transcend immeasurably even the most excellent of creatures' (O'Rourke 1992, p. 50).

This tension between apophasis and kataphasis, I want to argue, echoes and is echoed in considerations of the kinds of 'knowledge' it is possible to maintain about sex, gender and sexuality. Just as both knowing and unknowing further the project of understanding God even in God's ineffability – coming to know, in fact, that part of God's nature *is* to be unknown – so too bodies and identities can be recognized and endorsed in their knowability even as it is emphasized that their full significance is ultimately elusive. Body identities come to be figured as both self-constituting and as constituted by others in the community. Their genesis is thus both external and internal, as is their arena of signification. That bodies are known and unknown, that they are wholly irreducible yet at the same time wholly mysterious, is particularly significant given the ontological status of bodies in the Christian tradition. In the Eucharist, human bodies assimilate into themselves the body of Christ, thereby actually *becoming* the body of Christ, and perichoretically entering into all its other human members. Bodies thereby define themselves and define all other bodies.

---

5 O'Rourke says, 'With Aquinas the notion of being acquires an all-transcendent and infinite value. It is thus, he believes, the concept most appropriate to denote the infinity of God. And as an analogous notion, revealed in each reality, it is furthermore, the key to our reflection leading from beings to God. It is precisely as Being Itself, transcendent and unlimited ... that God is in himself radically unknown; by the same token it is also because he is Being that we have analogous knowledge of his existence, and relation with creatures. Thus, whereas for Dionysius it is a hindrance to our discovery of God that human knowledge is oriented toward finite beings, this for Aquinas is the very foundation of our natural disclosure of God' (O'Rourke 1992, p. 56). God is infinitely knowable, because God has infinite Being to be known; it is just that this is not apprehensible by the human intellect (O'Rourke 1992, p. 57).

This is especially important in considering transgender, given that gender dysphoria has often been figured as psychological disturbance, and transgendered people's agency in determining their own bodies has thereby been eroded. Jay Prosser famously comments that 'There are transsexuals who seek very pointedly to be nonperformative, to be constantive, quite simply, to *be*' (Prosser 1998, p. 32). To suppose that transsexualism is the only chosen, 'constructed' sex-gender identity, argues Prosser, both denies the constructed nature of *all* gender identity and further undermines the existence of the transsexual as a subject with agency, eroding 'the subject's capacity . . . to initiate and effect his/her own somatic transition' (Prosser 1998, p. 8). For Prosser, transgender is *not* always obviously 'queer' or subversive of heterosexual norms, but this does not render it illegitimate. Transgendered people *can* be self-constituting and claim a 'reality' in their bodily manifestations, and can indeed invest in this a heterosexual identity where the new identity is a site for eroticism directed at members of the individual's original sex. Incontrovertibly, transgendered people can know themselves and project themselves just as authentically as anyone else can. Importantly, however, as I explore below, this may come to occur even alongside an acknowledgement that human gender is an imperfect and penultimate construct which may not survive (at least in recognizable form) human transformation in the image of God. So transgendered people can *only* know and project themselves as authentically as anyone else can, that is, in an extensive but limited manner. It is not possible to say what God is, but only what God is not, as apophatic theologies have emphasized; similarly, it is not possible to say that transgender *is* (or should be) homonormative, but only that it is *not* unproblematically heteronormative, despite ostensibly echoing some patterns from heterosexual discourse (as that men should be 'masculine', that women should be 'feminine', and – sometimes – that men should have 'male' genitalia and women should have 'female' genitalia). Significantly, this knowing-unknowing tension begins to point to questions about the extent to which human gender is a necessary category at all, particularly for humans who recognize themselves as made in the image of God.

Apophatic Tensions?

Although apophatic theology has potential as a locus for dialogue with transgender, it is also necessary to acknowledge briefly the problem that, in some respects, apophasis might appear somewhat alien to transgender studies. The discourses which have sprung up around transgender, intersex and related issues have often been profoundly embodied, incarnational ones, valuing personal experience and testimony and questioning the scientific-academic norms which have said that these are not adequate or legitimate bases for knowledge. By contrast, Clement of Alexandria (for example) appeals to the negative or apophatic way largely because, like many later thinkers, he *rejects* knowledge acquired through sense perception (Hägg 2006, p. 213; cf. Rorem's reading of Pseudo-Dionysius in Rorem 1984, p. 89) and considers negative theological expression a way to sidestep it. This might appear very anti-incarnational, and thus in conflict with corporeal, physical ideals of knowledge. For Clement himself the problem is overcome by the fact that apophasis is only one strand of his thought about the possibility of knowing God; he, too, appeals, on the flip side, to kataphasis, or positive knowledge of God. Henny Fiskå Hägg says that, for Clement, 'both ways of approaching God, the negative and the positive, are equally true. The two ways to God are complementary, like a dialectical interrelationship of darkness and light' (Hägg 2006, p. 263). By analogy, we might say that it is important continually to explore the ways in which transgender expressions of identity are both *like* and *unlike* non-trans ones – both as a reminder that trans is only one element of human sex-gender identity, which cannot alone 'stand for' or 'symbolize' the provisionality of all such identity, and in order to emphasize that it is in all our tensions of likeness and unlikeness that we recognize ourselves as human.

Hägg notes Clement's influence on the Cappadocian fathers, who sought to retain these two forms of knowledge, positive and negative, so that God's essential nature would remain ineffable to humans (thus saving God from the risk of simply being subsumed either to being an object of human knowledge, or of being something solely of the same nature as humans) – but also, simultaneously, so that humans could know and participate in God (Hägg 2006, p. 265).[6] Here apophasis is emphasized as being a proactive unknowing, not a passive ignorance (Williams 2004, p. 191). It is thus not so unproblematically 'opposite' from active, positive kataphatic attempts to figure or 'find' God as it might first appear. Despite the claims of Rorem and others that Meister Eckhart (for example) actually rejects claims like the one that God *is* good (see Rorem 1984, pp. 143–4), it is possible to read this not as a claim that *nothing* can be known of God, but rather as a statement something like, 'All this *can* be known of God; yet God is also still more than all of it.' However, given that the kataphatic strand became the one so overemphasized in later Western Christianity (despite Aquinas' extensive use of the *via negativa*), which has not exactly thrown open its arms to embrace transgendered (and intersexed) bodies and their implications for its doctrines about sex, gender, sexuality and complementarity, it is worth being mettlesome on behalf of apophasis and its potential to disrupt unproblematized, rigidly demarcated structures of discourse – even if some of its historic proponents necessarily did not utilize it in the service of incarnational theology in the ways that we might now wish to emphasize.

Another possible problem in using apophatic theologies to reflect on transgender, in light of the ways in which apophasis has been used by the historical theologians, arises from Aquinas' belief that 'the names of all things may be spoken of [God]; but in the measure that they fail to represent him, we remove from God the names we have imposed and pronounce their opposites' (O'Rourke 1992, p. 51). This kind of strong binary thinking appears to be exactly what has led to the 'homonormativity' identified by Stryker, whereby the 'negation' of one set of oppressive norms is only 'legitimately' done by resisting them in a particular, specific way – which, if manifested for instance as enforced homonormativity or,

6 Janet P. Williams says of Pseudo-Dionysius, 'Dionysius' language is of the "beyondness" of God, not of transcendence as opposed to immanence; and therefore, in a typical paradox, the divine which is beyond all duality transcends even the duality of transcendence and immanence, is known in all created works, and called by every name' (Williams 2004, p. 188). If this is not queer it is, at least, profoundly liminal, refusing fixity or finality of description, and thereby defying narrowness of definition.

indeed, liminal gender, may itself exclude the experience of some transgendered people.

Importantly, however, as Fran O'Rourke emphasizes,

> All things may both be affirmed and denied of God, but truly speaking, [God] is beyond the operations of attribution and negation; these are characteristic of human reflection and cannot be brought to bear upon divine being, which in its excellence outmeasures the categories of human thought. Affirmation and negation, therefore, are not mutually exclusive for the very reason that neither is properly commensurate with the mystery of the divinity. God is most faithfully known not simply through negation, but as the unknown. (O'Rourke 1992, pp. 52–3)

This means that, although Aquinas rejects the potentially 'agnostic' character of Dionysius' thought (O'Rourke 1992, p. 55), the acknowledgement that God is unknown means that apophaticism in some form still has the potential to be used for promoting *variety and multiplicity* in the ways in which the heteronormative metanarrative are rejected. Affirmations and negations of God's nature are not enough; it is not just *what* can and cannot be known of God that matters, but exactly *that* God cannot be known as neatly as humans generally like to know. Similarly, as affirmation and negation are not mutually exclusive because neither is properly commensurate with the mystery of God, so 'heteronormativity' and 'homonormativity' are not mutually exclusive because neither is properly commensurate with the both-yet-neither character of transgender. Thus transgender may retain ostensibly 'heterosexual' and 'homosexual' echoes without thereby acting as an uncritical pawn for either side. For this reason, in our own context, all transgendered people need not come to be figured as inherently disturbing all human sex and gender just by existing, yet there *can* be an 'otherness' in transgender's relationship to both hetero- and homonormativity. This otherness is itself not single or monolithic, but rather represents the aspect of transgendered identity which is self-constituting and self-governing and may sometimes disseminate what appear to be conservative gender identities.

A Transformative Way through the Binaries

The apophatic element in the thought of the Cappadocian Gregory of Nyssa might be especially significant here – apophasis critiquing apophasis – in helping show how space might be carved out for specific transgendered identity in a barrenly binary landscape where even 'queer' sometimes seems exclusionary. Indeed, the apparently (so-called) 'gender-bending', 'transgendered' and more broadly disruptive tendency in some of Gregory's writings has been extensively explored elsewhere (see especially Nausner 2002 and Burrus 2007). For example, Sarah Coakley says, 'Gregory's gender theory, like Butler's, does not claim to obliterate the binaries that remain culturally normative, but seeks – also like Butler – to find a transformative way through them' (Coakley 2000, p. 67).

In fact, Gregory himself exhorts,

> Let us change in such a way that we may constantly evolve towards what is better, being transformed from glory to glory, and thus always improving and ever becoming more perfect by daily growth, and *never arriving at any limit of perfection*. For perfection consists in our *never stopping in our growth in good, never circumscribing our perfection by any limitation*. (Gregory of Nyssa, *On Perfection*, in Daniélou 1961, p. 84) (my emphasis)

Coakley calls this provisional, restless picture of perfection 'a daring move for a Platonist' (Coakley 2000, p. 68) and acknowledges that Gregory's ideas of gender 'reversal' undercut and subvert notions of traditional married gender roles. Importantly, though, in a contemporary setting, they also seem to undercut and subvert their common inversions as homonormative. They refuse any sense of 'arrival', rejecting a climactic picture of perfection in favour of a transformative one based on uncertainty and continual journeying. It is living in the tension, the often discomfiting uncertainty, that transforms us and promotes our growth as human.

Coakley shows that Gregory's picture of gender here is anti-essentialist

– and, perhaps, by extension, anti-heteronormative. But it is possible to read Gregory conservatively too; Coakley herself cites work by Verna Harrison, who asks whether perhaps Gregory actually reinforces gender binaries in his theological manoeuvrings. It is certainly possible to read Gregory as a gender traditionalist – as, for instance, in his apparent belief that virtue is a 'male' quality and vice a 'female' one (Burrus 2007, p. 153) even though he figures male and female symbolically rather than biologically. But Coakley, after Harrison, concludes that the point is that *eros*, gender and all other aspects of human identity come eventually in Gregory to be defined more and more by what they are *in God*. In other words, human binaries or either/or constructions are no longer adequate descriptions of what it is to be human. Ultimately, Harrison herself reads Gregory as finding human gender rather unimportant:

> Gregory sees gender as a secondary and temporary feature of the human condition. In this life it characterizes the body but not the soul, and in the next life it is displaced by properties imprinted by the deiform soul in its transfigured body. (Harrison 1990, p. 460)

Coakley expands:

> The message Gregory evidently wishes to convey is that gender stereotypes must be reversed, undermined, and transcended if the soul is to advance to supreme intimacy with the trinitarian God; and that the language of sexuality and gender, far from being an optional aside or mere rhetorical flourish in the process, is somehow necessary and intrinsic to the epistemological deepening that Gregory seeks to describe. (Coakley 2002, p. 128)

She adds, 'It is important to note that this gender-play bespeaks shifts in human epistemological *capacity* which cannot be gained except through painstaking spiritual growth' (Coakley 2002, p. 128). In other words, such gender-bending is necessary for human growth mainly because it reflects the gender fluidity in God (Coakley 2002, p. 128; Harrison 1996, p. 68) and expresses the *already existing* truth that in Christ there is 'neither male nor female' (so Coakley cites the text).[7] Going beyond humanly constructed binaries, then, is a difficult but possible move for humans to make; gender plays only 'a temporary and instrumental role' in the 'creative design' to be fulfilled in the *eschaton* (Harrison 1990, p. 468).

This might be a difficult thing to hear for transgendered people who have found claiming their gender, and perhaps having surgical intervention to reinforce their physical projection of it, to be an essential part of finding a comfortable and psychologically healthy identity. Gregory himself seems to want to reverse, undermine or transcend gender (Coakley 2002, pp. 127–9; Harrison 1990, 1996), but transgender might be said to reinforce it.[8] However, as we have seen, the 'otherness' of transgender is such that it is neither wholly like nor wholly unlike the socio-sexual phenomena which it echoes in some respects. Moreover, it must be acknowledged – as Harrison has shown – that gender is profoundly a *human* attribute. God is not gendered as humans are. It is crucial, therefore, that human gender is not taken to signify anything absolute about what God is (as has tended to happen when the common imagery of God

---

7 I prefer the translation 'no longer . . . male and female', particularly in contrast with 'Jew *or* Greek' and 'slave *or* free' earlier in the verse (Gal. 3.28). The placing of 'male and female' after two clauses grounded palpably in *social* meaning suggests that it is male-and-female as an exclusive, socially limiting construct, rather than male and female as two gamete possibilities among a range of other configurations, which pass away in Christ. What has ceased to be 'in Christ' is the all-embracing male-and-female schema for human existence: a restricted, heteronormative system wherein humans are made meaningful only in and through so-called sexual complementarity. There is thus space in the Galatians text for acknowledging the real existence of those who either are not 'sexed' at all in the binary system (such as some of those with physical intersex conditions) or have chosen to live out a more liminal identity.

8 Such is the claim, for example, of Sharon Preves, who argues that elective transsexual surgery may in fact affirm, rather than challenge, binary gender norms, rendering sex reassignment surgery part of what makes society at large so inhospitable to non-typical bodies (Preves 2003, pp. 45–6). This is particularly problematic from the perspective of intersex, says Preves, because transsexual transition supports the hegemony which insists that physical gender signifiers *must* match the lived gender in order for psychological well-being to persist. It thereby further erodes the bodily legitimacy of intersexed people.

as a father becomes over-naturalized); but, just as importantly, if humans image a genderless God, then gender is not an absolute or ultimate aspect of human identity either. This is the case *even if* apparently 'dualistic', 'heteronormative' or 'essentialist' gender identities are important for some transgendered people, since gender is just as much an important element of how we currently understand ourselves as it is an irrelevance in what we are becoming. As Rorem says of Dionysian apophasis, 'the conceptions gained . . . will themselves be negated eventually, not in yet another interpretation but in an abandonment entirely . . . to that which is ultimately transcendent' (Rorem 1984, p. 89).

Queer Acts I: The Ceding of Identity

Stryker expresses ambivalence about the usefulness of queer theories as sites for transgendered becoming, but the notion of the provisionality of human gender finds echoes in the queer-conscious theologies of our own day. Gerard Loughlin, for example, predicts that *all* 'identities' must be 'washed away in the baptismal waters', since 'they have no ultimacy in Christ' (Loughlin 2007a, pp. 12–13). Elizabeth Stuart holds that it is the Church's 'eschatological horizon' which demonstrates that gender and sexual identity cannot be of 'ultimate concern' (Stuart 2007, p. 65). Gender is a human quality that speaks to us of human limitedness and demarcation. We speak about and interact with God as gendered beings. But God Godself is not gendered in the way that humans are, so the part of us that is – to borrow Grace Jantzen's phrase – becoming divine is not necessarily a part that needs to maintain gender as a central or critical aspect of selfhood. We reflect the image of an indubitably genderless God, as well as all the gendered quasi-Gods of our own creation. As humans living in human societies it may still be appropriate to live out 'limited' human identities such as those grounded in binary gender; what is crucial is that it is accepted that this is a finite and penultimate aspect of being human. In order to know what it is to be *truly* human we may eventually have to let go of something that for many people seems the very essence of our humanity, our existence as gendered beings.

It is sometimes argued that straight-identified transgendered persons' particular temporary, human identities are reinforcing the narrowness of those roles and making it even more difficult for those who do, in fact, prefer more liminal or ambiguous expressions of gender. However, it is important to stress that this is a much broader issue impacting on *anyone* who claims a distinct gendered identity. Transgendered people who are simply trying to get by should in no way have to bear the responsibility of 'solving' it on behalf of everyone else. Indeed, many transgendered people embark on the process of surgical and hormonal transition precisely because of the social pressure to fit into either one narrow gender presentation category or its 'opposite'. It is exhausting constantly to encounter stares and interrogation because one's gender presentation is unusual; non-transgendered people do not usually face the same hostility or scrutiny about their gender presentations, even though they, just as much as 'straight' transgendered people, are part of the society that helps construct and reinforce particular gender norms. It could be argued that transgender, intersex and otherwise 'atypical' configurations inherently disrupt the heteronormative matrix, and that this is a good thing; but it could equally be argued that transgendered and intersexed people should not have to do so on behalf of everyone else, and that if a transgendered person needs to 'pass' in order to survive, that is no more reprehensible or apolitical than it would be for anyone else who gets to pass just because they have an apparently unremarkable sex-gender presentation and it never occurs to anyone to question them about it. This is why it is so important that, as Loughlin, Elizabeth Stuart (Stuart 2007, p. 65) and others comment, it is *all* identities that are penultimate. Those who are non-transgendered are called to recognize their gendered identities as provisional and temporary just as much as those who are transgendered.

This idea comes through particularly strongly in the work of the scholar of intersex Iain Morland. Morland himself holds that intersex and transgender identity politics are of different orders, for the reason that many intersexed individuals did not elect to have the surgery they have undergone – particularly, of course, those operated on in infancy and childhood. This fundamental distinction, he says, rests in the fact that, with intersex,

> The ability to identify one's sex has been fractured by surgery in a morally and physically injurious way that is irreparably prior to the desires and identifications of the individual in the present. In contrast, trans politics tends to centre on the realization of desires and identifications that are knowable to the trans individual, and which require merely social acknowledgement. (Morland [forthcoming] 2009).

Morland is right to distinguish between trans and intersex, since their conflation has been part of what has been deemed to erode the particularity of each group as they engage in the struggle for the governance of their own bodies. Even if there is a profound difference between their surgical histories, however, intersex can still speak to transgender in other ways. The 'mere' social acknowledgement which Morland suggests is all transgendered people need is not all that easy to come by, and is (as Spade has suggested [2006, p. 329]) often somewhat unimaginative in scope. This means that many trans people, like many intersexed people, may still find their capacity 'freely' to realize their sex-gender identity threatened – even though, as Morland emphasizes, the actual decision to undergo surgery is a choice which transgendered people have and many intersexed people who underwent surgical 'correction' as infants or children did not. For Morland, however, 'choice' goes beyond the 'unusually' sexed or gendered and is turned back on those whose identities are privileged with such 'normality' as to go unremarked. The impressive conclusion Morland reaches in his paper is that

> To the extent that an identity claim to be of a particular sex is an evaluative endorsement of a way of being treated, and of one's entitlement to behave in certain ways, the identity claims 'male' and 'female' cannot be appropriate, because they endorse and perpetuate one's access to unjust privileges. (Morland [forthcoming] 2009)

For this reason, he claims, non-intersexed people should relinquish the identities 'male' and 'female', for the reason that descriptivism is itself a value-system – one which 'devalues intersex'; so descriptivism itself 'should be devalued, via the repudiation of those identity claims that reinforce it' (Morland [forthcoming] 2009).

Morland is not a theologian, but this move of his speaks profoundly into the theological issue of *kenosis*, a self-emptying of what I have said, after Morland, is the indefensible privilege attached to unambiguous sex. As I have remarked in response to an earlier version of Morland's argument, and in light of Paul's injunction to honour the weaker members of the body in 1 Corinthians 12,

> If it is considered 'weak' to lack a particular sexed status, then, rather than making those who lack binary sexed status the exception and compensating for them on these grounds, why not make it that *everyone else* cedes the 'honour' attached to unambiguously sexed status? Just as embracing disabled bodies entails a conceptual shift so that 'healing' need not mean 'becoming able-bodied', so embracing the 'weaker' or less honoured members of the sexual body might mean ceding perceived 'goods' such as unambiguous sex. (Cornwall 2008, p. 188)

To promote the ceding of certain identity to those transgendered people who may have struggled long to 'pass', or to feel that they have finally come to a place of peace with their own body identities, may in itself seem problematic. It may seem of the same order as counselling kenotic, self-denying behaviour to victims of domestic violence, or to other groups who have traditionally been encouraged far too much to give over their autonomy (as Daphne Hampson has discussed in Hampson 1990, p. 155; and 1996, pp. 129–30). Indeed, I am not suggesting that trans people should have to give up the privileges and securities attached to passing as masculine men or feminine women any more than anyone else should. What is crucial in Morland's argument is that he wants the ceding of 'descriptivist privilege' to be undergone primarily by the *non*-intersexed, that is, by those who do *not* have unusual configurations of sex and gender.

I have suggested elsewhere that

> To cling to a particular model of human gender because it is thought to be central to human status as being in the image of God is not only

> unhelpful – as Morland implies – but also idolatrous. For humans to cling solely to what they already believe to be true of God can only limit a fuller understanding of what it is actually possible to know of God . . . The 'kenotic hymn' of Phil. 2.5–11 counsels that humans are to emulate Jesus, who did not consider equality with God something to be grasped; but to exploit, to cling, or to grasp at equality with God is exactly what is happening when humans decide that a single . . . reading of gender tells the whole story of God. (Cornwall 2008, p. 189)

And so we reach a double-edged implication: accepting the provisionality and penultimacy of human constructs of sex and gender must be done first and foremost by those who have the most to lose as a consequence, as an eschatological-prophetic act of solidarity with those often made marginal because of their body identities. This may mean doing everything possible to make this a world where transgendered people can fully live in their own most veritable expressions of gender identity – even where it may seem to bolster binaristic, heterosexist norms – while simultaneously working to bring about a world where clear, unambiguous gender identities are rather unimportant. At the next level, and as the *eschaton* comes to be more fully anticipated and realized, then, leaving gender behind may *also* be a vital step for those in whom the recognition of their self-identified gender has been an important aspect of their journey toward fuller, more integrated personhood. It is unlikely that this will occur while the majority of human social systems and discourses are still set up to privilege a dualistic, binary-sexed-and-gendered world, but it is an ardent hope for those who would become Godlike in terms of nurturing God's own multiplicity, liminality and presence in real, imperfect human lives.

Queer Acts II: Resisting Finality

In commenting on how Gregory of Nyssa employs strikingly free, instrumental imagery for the Trinity in his exegesis, rather than appealing to philosophical precision (Coakley 2002, p. 122), Coakley suggests,

'[Gregory] . . . wishes us not to fixate on one set of images, but to allow all of them to be permeated by the profoundly apophatic sensibility that propels us from one to the other' (Coakley 2002, p. 123). As we have seen, perfection in this account means never having arrived, never giving in to the human desire to categorize, demarcate and control recalcitrant phenomena. This might also entail a continual disruption and querying of all our narrative discourses, whether they appear to be working in the service of currently dominant norms or not. The existence of transgendered people who do not identify with the specifically homosexual or (in Stryker's reading) 'queer' version of anti-heteronormativity confirms rather than negates the multitudinous phalanx of possibilities engendered in human identity and in God. This does not mean that we must not continue to question and query precisely *which* configurations and patterns of relationship are more-or-less loving, freeing and just; but to assume that 'straight' transgendered people are 'letting the side down', because they too unproblematically endorse heteronormativity, fails to look for the subversive choices and statements being made by non-transgendered heterosexual people too.

This continual querying of norms is what has already begun to happen, and must continue to happen, within queer discourse. Unlike Stryker, I do not believe queer always tends to gaycentrism or homonormativity. In fact, queer theologies in particular have the potential to continue to acknowledge as provisional *all* human constructs. Crucially, commented Butler in *Bodies That Matter*, 'queer' must be recognized as a profoundly contingent term, which must be allowed to take on meanings beyond those anticipated by people for whom it carries specific and limited political meaning. She says,

> That it can become such a discursive site whose uses are not fully constrained in advance ought to be safeguarded not only for the purposes of continuing to democratize queer politics, but also to expose, affirm, and rework the specific historicity of the term. (Butler 1993, p. 230)

The expansion of queer (particularly within queer theologies) in the last decade – explicitly to include models and sites of subversion not specifically located in lesbian and gay discourse, and thereby to resonate with expressions of transgender which are neither fully like nor fully unlike heteronormative sex-gender configurations – is *already* the revision mooted by Butler. This need not be read as a false homogenization negating the particularity of different groups' struggles, an accusation sometimes levelled at queer and which seems to lie behind Stryker's assertion about homonormativity; it rather represents a blossoming of multiplicity with justice and fullness of personhood as central, common ends. As such, queer must be continually reframed and reworked. It is profoundly eschatological: transformative and transforming, provisional, its meaning constantly made and remade, done and undone. Some scholars of transgender may be suspicious of queer studies, but it is precisely in 'queer' aspects of the theological tradition that apophasis is found and endorsed and in which the quashing binaries of homonormativity–heteronormativity can be sidestepped. Virginia Burrus comments that the momentum of repetition itself, central to existing in a tradition with which many queer theologians have expressed ambivalence 'ensures, for better and for worse, that no word is final' (Burrus 2007, p. 148). This includes the 'finality' of human gender, whether read as something constant and unchanging (as by many transgendered people who deem that it is their bodies which may be altered to reflect a gender identity which has always been the same, despite not 'matching' the erstwhile body) or as something shifting and performed.

Theology's relationship to other modes of discourses is unique; ideally, it points beyond human ideology altogether, to a God profoundly involved with human existence but not limited or quashed by it. Because of their capacity to query all ideologies – not just heteronormative ones – and because of their insistence that all human ideology is provisional or penultimate, queer theologies, promote a resisting attitude toward oppressive ideologies. Queer theologies hold within themselves a tension between the fulfilled and the partial, the completed and the ever incomplete. These kinds of tensions, the tensions between absence and presence, difference and affinity, distance and proximity have been traced throughout the theological tradition (as, persuasively, by Graham Ward in two post-resurrection accounts of Jesus' interactions with Mary

Magdalene and Thomas the Twin – Ward 2007). Queer theologies, then, if reflecting what David M. Halperin traces as the necessary quality for queer politics, namely, that they be 'anchored in the perilous and shifting sands of non-identity, positionality, discursive reversibility, and collective self-invention' (Halperin 1995, p. 122), have the potential to overcome some of the binaries entrenched in heteronormative discourse in general. This may be grounded in Christian tradition, *despite* some of the profoundly oppressive and abusive uses to which it has been put, given Tim Gorringe's claim that 'what allows us to speak of "revelation" with regard to the Christian Scriptures is their continuing capacity to challenge our taken for granted pieties' (Gorringe 2004, p. 172). No human authority can be taken as ultimate; no human system can be unproblematically bettered by its 'opposite', since its opposite will still be imperfect. Homonormativity cannot be the whole answer to the problem of heteronormativity. Since apophasis means never having arrived at the limits of perfection or of understanding, no human project and no human identity – including gendered identity – may be said to put the final word on what it is to be a human being made in the image of a not-yet-knowable God.

Conclusions

Much of the value of apophasis for reading transgender, then, may lie simply in its capacity to endorse multiplicity even where this is discomfiting. For those who have rejected a narrative rooted in binary gender, the desire of some transgendered people to 'pass' can be disquieting. It may seem utterly antithetical that one should endorse the 'heteronormative' expressions of gender so desired by some transgendered people while simultaneously suggesting that it would be better if a binary-gendered system did not exist – and that there may be a hope for a future where such a system in fact no longer holds reign. But there is many a precedent for querying an ideology from the 'inside' in order to bring about its downfall more effectively. In Alan Paton's short story 'Debbie Go Home', set in 1950s South Africa under apartheid, the local Mothers' Club organizes a Debutantes' Ball where young black girls will be received by the white

Administrator and his wife. Jim de Villiers's teenaged daughter Janie has been invited and her mother wants her to go, but de Villiers and his militant student son, Johnny, are not in favour. In fact, Johnny and his friends are planning to picket the ball. However, Mrs de Villiers persuades Johnny that Janie should be allowed to go to the ball even though Johnny will be protesting there – in order that she might have just 'one night, in a nice dress and the coloured lights . . . And for one night the young men will be wearing gloves, and bowing to her as gentlemanly as you like, not pawing at her in some dark yard' (Paton 1961, p. 16). It is de Villiers who has to give permission for Janie to go, however, and anxious not to upset his mother any more, and in an apparently radical turnaround, it is eventually Johnny who makes the bargain with his father, agreeing to help him write a speech to give at a union meeting only on condition that Janie be allowed to attend the ball.

> 'All right, she can go,' [de Villiers] said, 'on one condition. Tell me how you justify it.'
>
> 'Rock-bottom necessity,' said Johnny. 'If I boycott American food, and I'm dying of hunger, and everywhere around me is American food, then I eat American food.'
>
> 'You eat American food so you can go on boycotting it,' said de Villiers. (Paton 1961, p. 21)

One eats American food so one can go on boycotting it; perhaps it is sometimes also appropriate that one echoes 'heterosexual' patterns in order to carry on critiquing them. And in the meantime, in the 'passing', one might be treated with more respect and dignity than those who differ in more actively oppositional ways. However, it is also important to acknowledge that such safety may be only temporary – may be only 'one night' of dresses and dancing and lights – and that it may be only a preliminary step on the way to more drastic change in social and political systems. But given that apophasis fundamentally gives space to *not* know, to have *not* reached our 'destination', this allows us to tread a path where such diversity and 'at-once-ness' – such apparent contradiction – does not immediately have to be resolved. Apophasis reinforces the provisionality of all human gender constructs, shedding light on an aspect of the Christian tradition which can be read as profoundly valuing process over *telos*, journey over arrival.

The kinds of tensions identified by Ward – between absence and presence, difference and affinity, distance and proximity – exist too in the tensions in the transgendered body itself. It is transformative, because it speaks to the non-ultimacy of traditional sex-gender-sexuality configurations, but it must also be further transformed. Ward concludes that 'the meaning and significance of bodies is ultimately ungraspable. Their givenness cannot be accounted for . . . and they cannot account for themselves (as empiricists would like us to believe)' (Ward 2007, p. 84). Importantly, says Ward, bodies are always in transit, exceeding whatever they appear to be at a given time. Embodiment itself is – paradoxically – transcorporeal (Ward 2007, p. 84). To be a discrete body, then, whether one which appears to subvert or appears to endorse established sex-gender-sexuality norms, is always already to be constructed by others as well as being self-constructing and self-projecting. There is something irreducible about bodies as accidents of flesh and blood, but bodies are also always multiplicitous because of their interrelatedness to other bodies and stories. There is thus a perpetual tightrope to be trod between what bodies are in and of themselves and what they mean as signifiers of overall human bodiliness (which is almost synonymous with human existence).

Apophasis, in the work of Gregory of Nyssa, Pseudo-Dionysius and others, claims *all* human imagery as insufficient, since this circumvents the possibility of 'superseding' one inadequate image with another equally deficient one. This resonates strongly with Stryker's rejection of the 'homonormativity' which she senses from some queer quarters, on the grounds that transgender need not be unproblematically 'homosexual' in order to interrogate and subvert heteronormative hegemonies effectively, and echoes the apophatic theological claim that it is not possible to know what God is, but only what God is not. Rejecting heteronormative models and discourses must not prescribe unreflectively 'homonormative' alternatives. It is for this reason that, for us as humans as well as in our expressions about God, it is only possible to say what we are not. Transgendered people often desire a clear expression of gender which is unambiguously and unremarkably understood by others. In this they are far from alone. Human gender is important. However, it is not ultimate. Our gender identities are not the final word about us; they are part of our becoming but they are not the becoming itself, which is always ahead, always beyond, always delayed. We have, indeed, not reached the limits of our perfection.

References

Burrus, Virginia (2007), 'Queer Father: Gregory of Nyssa and the Subversion of Identity', in Gerard Loughlin, ed. (2007b), *Queer Theology: Rethinking the Western Body* (Oxford: Blackwell), pp. 147–62.

Butler, Judith (1993), *Bodies That Matter: On the Discursive Limits of 'Sex'* (New York and London: Routledge).

Coakley, Sarah (2000), 'The Eschatological Body: Gender, Transformation and God', *Modern Theology* 16.1, pp. 61–73.

Coakley, Sarah (2002), *Powers and Submissions: Spirituality, Philosophy and Gender* (Oxford: Blackwell).

Cornwall, Susannah (2008), 'The *Kenosis* of Unambiguous Sex in the Body of Christ: Intersex, Theology and Existing "for the Other"', *Theology & Sexuality* 14.2, pp. 181–99.

Devore, Howard (1999), 'Growing Up in the Surgical Maelstrom', in Alice Domurat Dreger, ed., *Intersex in the Age of Ethics* (Hagerstown, MD: University Publishing Group), pp. 78–81.

Dreger, Alice Domurat (1998), *Hermaphrodites and the Medical Invention of Sex* (Massachusetts and London: Harvard University Press).

Dreger, Alice Domurat, ed. (1999), *Intersex in the Age of Ethics*, Hagerstown, MD: University Publishing Group.

Evans, G. R., ed. (2004), *The First Christian Theologians: An Introduction to Theology in the Early Church* (Oxford: Blackwell).

Gorringe, T. J. (2004), *Furthering Humanity: A Theology of Culture* (Aldershot: Ashgate).

Hägg, Henny Fiskå (2006), *Clement of Alexandria and the Beginnings of Christian Apophaticism* (Oxford: Oxford University Press).

Halperin, David M. (1995), *Saint Foucault: Towards a Gay Hagiography* (New York and Oxford: Oxford University Press).

Hampson, Daphne (1990), *Theology and Feminism* (Oxford: Blackwell).

Hampson, Daphne (1996), 'On Power and Gender', in Adrian Thatcher and Elizabeth Stuart, eds, *Christian Perspectives on Sexuality and Gender* (Leominster: Gracewing), pp. 125–40.

Harrison, Verna E. F. (1990), 'Male and Female in Cappadocian Theology', *Journal of Theological Studies* 41, pp. 441–71.

Harrison, Verna E. F. (1996), 'Gender, Generation and Virginity', *Journal of Theological Studies* 47, pp. 38–68.

Loughlin, Gerard (2007a), 'Introduction: The End of Sex', in Gerard Loughlin, ed., *Queer Theology: Rethinking the Western Body* (Oxford: Blackwell), pp. 1–34.

Loughlin, Gerard, ed.(2007b), *Queer Theology: Rethinking the Western Body* (Oxford: Blackwell).

Morland, Iain (forthcoming 2009), 'Why Five Sexes Are Not Enough', in Noreen Giffney and Michael O'Rourke, eds, *The Ashgate Research Companion to Queer Theory* (Aldershot: Ashgate).

Nausner, Michael (2002), 'Toward Community Beyond Gender Binaries: Gregory of Nyssa's Transgendering as Part of His Transformative Eschatology', *Theology & Sexuality* 16, pp. 55–65.

O'Rourke, Fran (1992), *Pseudo-Dionysius and the Metaphysics of Aquinas* (Leiden: E. J. Brill).

Paton, Alan (1961), *Debbie Go Home* (London: Jonathan Cape).

Preves, Sharon E. (2003), *Intersex and Identity: The Contested Self* (New Brunswick, NJ; London: Rutgers University Press).

Prosser, Jay (1998), *Second Skins: The Body Narratives of Transsexuality* (New York: Columbia University Press).

Rorem, Paul (1984), *Biblical and Liturgical Symbols within the Pseudo-Dionysian Synthesis* (Toronto: Pontifical Institute of Mediaeval Studies).

Spade, Dean (2006), 'Mutilating Gender', in Susan Stryker and Stephen Whittle, eds, *The Transgender Studies Reader* (New York and London: Routledge), pp. 315–32.

Stryker, Susan (2004), 'Transgender Studies: Queer Theory's Evil Twin', *GLQ* 10.2, pp. 212–15.

Stryker, Susan (2006), '(De)subjugated Knowledges: An Introduction to Transgender Studies', in Susan Stryker and Stephen Whittle, eds, *The Transgender Studies Reader* (New York and London: Routledge), pp. 1–17.

Stryker, Susan and Stephen Whittle, eds (2006), *The Transgender Studies Reader* (New York and London: Routledge).

Stuart, Elizabeth (2007), 'Sacramental Flesh', in Gerard Loughlin, ed., *Queer Theology: Rethinking the Western Body* (Oxford: Blackwell), pp. 65–75.

Ward, Graham (2007), 'There Is No Sexual Difference', in Gerard Loughlin, ed., *Queer Theology: Rethinking the Western Body* (Oxford: Blackwell), pp. 76–85.

Williams, Janet P. (2004), 'Pseudo-Dionysius and Maximus the Confessor', in G. R. Evans, ed., *The First Christian Theologians: An Introduction to Theology in the Early Church* (Oxford: Blackwell), pp. 186–200.

2

Christian Experience as a Transsexual

HANNAH BUCHANAN

I was brought up in a Christian home by my mother who was a single parent. She was Church of Scotland and a Sunday school teacher. I attended Sunday school in a carefree way. When we moved to Yorkshire, I attended Beverley Minster, a beautiful cathedral type church in a lovely Yorkshire town. I knew I loved God, but like most young people I was fairly flippant about it.

However, it wasn't until I hit my teens that my faith took hold of me and I began to enter into what some describe as a 'relationship' with God.

For some time, I attended a large evangelical church in Winchester. However, I was at the age now where I was also beginning to question and challenge my faith.

I began to realize also, that this church (and later others like it) had very dogmatic, almost iron-bar-like views on certain core issues such as marriage, sexuality and the roles of men and women in society. Although I wasn't living as female at this point, I already had experience of what it was like to be different from the norm through my physical disability.

The church I attended was very evangelical, and it all seemed a bit too sanctimonious and self-serving for my liking. They seemed to be very zealous and excited at the prospect of their own passport to heaven, but very disinterested in how to bring in others, or treat non-Christians with equal respect.

So having become very cynical, I left that church. I was visited at home by members of the congregation and youth group leaders who told me I was making a big mistake and I'd probably go to hell.

You'd think I'd learn my lesson there wouldn't you? Well, I didn't.

I went to university at Oxford Brookes in 2000 to study English and Sociology. For a number of years after the Christ Church disaster, I hadn't attended a church at all.

In the first few weeks of my time at Brookes, I met a fresher called Ryan. We got talking, and it became apparent that Ryan was a Christian. He invited me along to one of the major churches in Oxford, also evangelical, St Aldates. Now to be honest, after my issues with Christ Church, I was pretty unenthusiastic about going. So, I didn't, bowing instead to pressure from my flatmates and carers who told me I didn't need 'god-squadders' in my life.

So it goes on. I didn't go to church until halfway through my second year at university. I'd had problems with an abusive carer just previously, so was feeling pretty low and vulnerable, not to mention depressed.

I thought that going to church might help. So, I remembered the name of the Church that Ryan had told me about, St Aldates. I looked online to see if they had a website to check for disabled access and practical things. They did, and it was easily reachable via bus to the city centre.

So, I went that evening. It seemed friendly and welcoming enough, with lively music and lots of young people. There were regular occurrences of people falling on the floor, and crying uncontrollably after services. This, according to the clergy, was the Holy Spirit at work.

But what I liked about this church was the large congregation; it was so enormous that I could just lose myself in it. There were also regular baptism services, mainly comprised of candidates who, it seems now, had done terrible things and then found St Aldates.

It was a good job I could lose myself, because parallel to this I was coming to terms with my sexuality. I had always identified with the more feminine, girly aspects of life, and naively thought that this made me gay, as in homosexual male.

So, this was the box I put myself in. I joined the LGBT Society (lesbian, gay, bisexual and transgender), made friends with everyone, donned the odd feather boa, and partied to cheesy music.

But back at St Aldates, it was the proposed ordination of Jeffrey John as Bishop of Reading that was the straw that broke the camel's back.

Now Jeffrey was openly gay, had been in a gay relationship for some thirty years, but had abstained from sex so, according to Church of England guidance, had done nothing wrong.

However, St Aldates were utterly opposed to the appointment, and I found myself feeling uncomfortable and almost persecuted. The rector even devoted a sermon to biblical texts which, in the eyes of St Aldates, proved that homosexuality was against Christian principles, and telling the congregation why St Aldates were opposed to the appointment.

Now in the end, Jeffrey's appointment as Bishop of Reading did not go ahead, but he became Dean of St Albans instead.

Sometime later, the Archbishop of Canterbury Dr Rowan Williams came to preach. He preached a perfectly interesting sermon, but there was a question-and-answer session. The rector put his hand up and began to tell the Archbishop how very disappointed St Aldates were by Jeffrey John's appointment in St Albans.

I leaned across to my carer and told her I couldn't listen to any more. With that, I left the service at very high speed.

So no church again for a while, that is until the last attempt at conforming, brought about by disabled toilet evangelism.

I was partying like a cheesy thing at GLAM, the university's cheesy themed student night, when I met this very friendly girl. Her name was Maria, she'd lived in Nepal and she was studying Occupational Therapy. We chatted about many things that night, but the conversation took an unexpected turn when she offered to help me to the toilet.

I went in, did what I had to do, and then she began to engage me in a conversation about attending church. I saw nothing of her for a few weeks, apart from the occasional text, asking me if I was coming to church.

In the end she turned up to take me to the Wednesday Bible group, FOCUS, held at the local school.

Now, around this time, I'd also been receiving counselling, abandoned my gay phase, and come to the conclusion that I was transsexual.

As soon as I entered the Bible group, something became apparent. There was a gender divide. The individual sub-groups were single sex. So I began feeling more of a hypocrite than ever before. While the men discussed their weaknesses regarding pornography and money, I had half an ear on the discussions about romance and women's roles within the Church, and the other trying desperately to fit in with 'the boys'.

My only short-term relief from this came when we used to escape over to the Sports Bar for drinks after the meetings. I then got to sit with the girls and chat. I felt more comfortable with this. That was frowned upon, however, and questions were asked. I was even asked if I felt less of a man because of my disability. I told them I was gay to keep them quiet. This for them was satisfactory, as long as I wasn't practising.

Eventually the pain of being a fraud was becoming too much. Leading a double life, I was out with the LGBT society on a Saturday and in church on Sundays. I was also growing closer to Maria and the other girls, and they treated me like one of them. But I didn't have to take any action myself this time, to leave.

My degree was ending and I came back to Hampshire to live at John Darling Mall, a hostel for physically disabled adults, while still keeping in touch with Maria and the others by telephone.

But soon after, I found a therapist, and began living as female. This is when my friendship with Maria and the others came to an abrupt end when I disclosed my true self to them.

They all urged me not to believe the lies, and told me that God's grace was sufficient enough for me to carry on living as male. They even mentioned my DNA!

I ignored them, however, and to this day they have ignored me, bar one of them, funnily enough also called Hannah.

I think that to understand the predicament of the transsexual we need look no further than Jesus. He was ridiculed, and marginalized. He reached out to Mary, allowing her to wash his hair. Jesus commanded us to love our neighbours as ourselves, with no discriminatory opt-outs.

Romans tells us that there is 'no condemnation in Christ Jesus' (Rom. 8.1). If this is so, why then am I condemned for my decision to honour myself as a woman in Christ? Clearly, I am not. The only right answer to this question is that humankind condemned me instead.

The other important question is, of course, did God create transsexuality? I think unequivocally yes 'definitely', if he created everything else.

Making u-turns in your life does not mean that everything will be perfect, nor easier, just different, as the Revd Dawson B. Taylor points out in a sermon preached at the Cathedral of Hope.

I definitely feel more fulfilled, and more real now, even if I have lost many 'friends'.

Those friendships were based on lies anyway, and a last desperate attempt by me to conform and fit in with society.

But I think it was still a useful experience, in that it forced my hand and made me admit my true feelings. I believe that, in order to know what you are, you must also know what you are not. I think the single-sex Bible study was God's way of showing me. It was the first time I had really had to try, badly, to take on the male role in society.

People often ask me what attracted me to evangelical churches, and what kept me going back for more.

I think they appear to be very welcoming places, with a snake charm-esque feeling, and very seductive and happy, that is until you put a toe out of line or say something controversial.

My Christian experience as a transsexual has been less disappointing overall than my experience *of* Christians as a transsexual. I know that God is still there, and God is with me always. However, in a fallen world the same cannot be said of my supposed Christian friends. I pray that their hearts will be opened, and their minds illuminated.

As to grace, finally, the greatest irony is that the central planks of the evangelical argument against transsexuality can also be taken to be in favour of it. If God's grace is sufficient enough for them to remain male, it is therefore also abundantly sufficient to allow them to be themselves.

3

We Come Bearing Gifts: Seven Lessons Religious Congregations Can Learn from Transpeople

VIRGINIA RAMEY MOLLENKOTT

We are living at a time when a 15-year-old boy was shot to death for wearing eye shadow and high heels to school, and for expressing his attraction to a boy a year younger than himself (*Advocate* 8 April 2008, pp. 29–33). It is also a time when a transman, now legally male and married to a woman, is six-months pregnant with a healthy baby girl (*Advocate* 8 April 2008, p. 24), and a time when ordained transpeople in the ministry are often punished for transitioning by congregational transfers involving huge pay-cuts, or even by loss of their credentials and livelihoods. It is high time for religious congregations to study gender issues, to wake up to the importance of noticing and embracing their transgender members, and to reach out in ministry with the transgender community as a whole.

In her book entitled *Our Tribe*, the Revd Elder Nancy Wilson writes about the three magi who brought their gifts to the baby Jesus. She comments that it is highly doubtful that they were kings, but quite possible that they were queens – and probably eunuchs and shamans. My guess is that they were people who today would be termed transwomen. I mention the magi because they are so important to the religious significance of Bethlehem, and because they symbolize the many gifts that transpeople of faith have to offer to any congregation that will receive us.

My plan here is first to list the seven major lessons that religious congregations could learn from their transgender members. Following the list, I shall explain and provide evidence for each of the lessons. There are many other things that could be said about why faith-congregations need transpeople, but seven lessons seem to me as much as I can adequately cover in the space I have been given.

Here are the seven lessons. First, any faith-congregation that honours the Bible should also honour transgender people because both the Hebrew and Christian Scriptures are extraordinarily transgender friendly. The gift here is that congregations will be empowered to see the Bible with a whole new perspective. Second, transpeople will assist congregations in transcending gender stereotypes that alienate men from women and from their own bodies, and oppress women and girls all over the world. Third, the transgender presence is a constant reminder of human diversity and hence of the much-needed diversity in religious language about God, the divine mystery that is beyond human imaginings and limitations. Fourth, until our recent cultural blindness, transpeople were always recognized as being specially gifted at building bridges between the seen and the unseen worlds, time and eternity; and many still carry that ability. Fifth, transpeople have by the circumstances of our lives been forced to become specialists in the connections between gender, sexuality, spirituality and justice, and many congregations are in desperate need of our assistance in making those connections. Sixth, because we embody 'the forgotten middle-ground' or 'ambiguity', transpeople can help to heal religious addictions to certainty – addictions that are threatening the survival of our entire planet. And seventh, transpeople incarnate the concept that just as all races are 'one blood', all genders and sexualities are 'one continuum' – and that the one blood and one continuum are sacred, made in the holy, divine image.

Now we turn to the evidence: first, the evidence that the Hebrew and Christian Scriptures are so transgender friendly that any congregation that claims to honour and obey biblical principles would need to embrace transpeople. There is a trend toward inclusiveness of sexual and gender minorities in the Bible: for instance, Deuteronomy 23.1 bans eunuchs (today's intersexuals, or also post-operative transwomen) from entering the temple, but Isaiah 56.4–5 welcomes eunuchs, Jesus praises them (Matt. 19.12), and the Ethiopian eunuch is promptly baptized (Acts 8.26–

9). Furthermore, Deuteronomy 22.5 forbids cross-dressing, but Romans 13.12 and 14 encourage spiritual cross-dressing, and Epimenides, a cross-dressing and homoerotic shaman, is quoted favourably in Acts 17.28 and Titus 1.12–13.

Genesis 2 depicts Adam as a hermaphroditic (intersexual) Earth Creature, later divided into the human male and female, while Genesis 1.27 states that both male and female are made in the image of the One Creator, who is thus depicted as androgynous (or 'transing' human gender). Accordingly, in addition to imagery of the holy one as male, both testaments also include imagery of God as female: giving birth, Holy Wisdom (Sophia), bakerwoman God, and so forth (Mollenkott 1983). The point, of course, is not that God is literally either male or female, but encompasses *both*, as well as all the in-between areas represented in the created universe.

If Matthew 1.23–5 is read literally, the virgin birth of Jesus was a parthenogenetic birth. In that case, 'he' was chromosomally female; yet according to Gospel accounts he was phenotypically male. (The male appearance, science tells us, can occur through a late-term sex reversal.) So anyone who takes the virgin birth literally must acknowledge that Jesus was intersexual (a form of transgenderism), and thus a perfect incarnation of the entire sex/gender continuum. Accordingly, an early baptismal formula, Galatians 3.28, testifies that in Christ 'there is no longer male and female'. For further details on the science of all of this see Kessel 1983.

Finally, the Christian Scriptures contain many transsexual images: women are called brothers; men are called the brides of Christ; Jesus and Paul are depicted as mothers (John 16.21; 17.1; and Gal. 4.19); Jesus is depicted as Holy Sophia (Wisdom); the Church is described as a female body with a male head (Eph. 5.23–33), and the female body of Christ is urged to grow up and become the male head (Eph. 4.15).

Circling back to the Old Testament, the name used for God in Genesis 17, El Shaddai, can mean 'the many-breasted one'. And if circumcision is a form of symbolic castration then, as Michael Carden has pointed out, 'To be in a covenant with the androgynous El Shaddai, Abraham and his male descendents are symbolically marked as eunuchs' (Carden 2006,

p. 35). In other words, circumcision marks Jewish men as symbolic transpeople.

The Jewish feminist scholar Judith Plaskow points out that the rabbis have always tolerated 'a certain range of gender ambiguity' because they did not want directly to clash with society's gender dimorphism. But now Dr Plaskow is calling Jews to 'dismantle [the traditional] binary gender construct', to move 'beyond the gender binary' by embracing transpeople of all sorts: transsexuals, cross-dressers, drag kings and queens, bi-gender people who are one gender at work and another at home, intersexuals, gays, lesbians, bisexuals who are transgressively gendered, and heterosexual masculine women and feminine men – indeed, anyone who 'has rebelled against traditional gender stereotypes and refused to accommodate to them'. Plaskow asserts, and I agree, that 'heterosexism and homophobia [and I would add, sexism itself] cannot finally be overcome without moving beyond the gender binary' (Plaskow 2007, p. 30).

One final piece of evidence from the New Testament: in Matthew 5.22, Jesus warns that 'anyone who calls his brother *Racha* shall be in danger of the council'. *Racha*, a non-Greek word, was a total mystery until 1934, when an ancient Egyptian papyrus was published that used *Racha* in reference to a particular person. The context in that papyrus indicates that the word *Racha* is equivalent to the Greek word *malakos*, meaning 'effeminate' (Roscoe 2004, p. 200). So Jesus was apparently warning against mockery of men who do not meet the traditional standards of masculinity – people who are 'genderqueer' or transgender.

I trust that by now I have provided sufficient evidence so that any reasonably open-minded person would have to agree that, once we take off our cultural blinders, both the Hebrew and Christian Scriptures are extraordinarily transgender friendly. An openly transgender presence will keep congregations aware of that fact.

Second, I have asserted that transpeople's open presence will assist congregations in overcoming the gender stereotypes that alienate men from women and from their own bodies, and oppress women and girls all over the world. As the masculine-but-female mother of a son whom I dearly love, I resent boys being told that 'real men don't cry' and 'real men are always in control of every situation'. Apparently even the apostle

Paul believed that cultural lie, because he wrote in Ephesians 5.29 that 'no man ever yet hated his own flesh'. But I have heard of men who have justified battering their wives by saying, 'The Bible says her bones and her flesh are one with mine, and I can break my own bones whenever I want to.' Around the world, women perform most of the hard labour but often receive only whatever food is left after the men have eaten. In Africa, thousands of women are dying of AIDS because they have no right to refuse unprotected sex with husbands who are HIV+. Such facts reveal that the binary gender construct does not merely *differentiate* men from women, it *elevates* men above women. But because we transgender people combine male and female traits in a multitude of ways, we offer visual, embodied assistance in laying aside such unjust perceptions and practices.

Third, transpeople are constant reminders of human diversity and hence will serve as constant reminders that our language concerning divinity needs to be diverse as well. Years ago, the then Roman Catholic philosopher Mary Daly wrote that 'If God is male, then the male is God.' And when I served on the National Council of Churches Inclusive Language Lectionary Committee, the news reporters could not believe that any of their contemporaries would actually think God is male. So we sent them out on the streets of New York City to ask people about the gender of God, and watched the results on the nightly news. Everybody referred to God as 'he' and of course had a male image to go with that pronoun. But transpeople have paid a high price for their awareness that maleness and femaleness, masculinity and femininity, are not necessarily tied to a person's genitalia. Therefore transpeople are sensitive to the injustices and oppressions that arise when some people are considered more sacred, more perfect and more entitled than other people. Transpeople are not tied to what Daniel Maguire calls 'pelvic orthodoxy'. So we are a people who are needed to remind religious congregations not only of human diversity but also of the fact that all of us in all our diversity are made in the image of one dazzlingly diverse Spirit. If we insist that congregational worship must reflect that dazzling diversity, we shall be doing justice toward the entire human race and the natural creation as well.

Fourth, until our heavily androcentric cultural assumptions blinded society to the realities of gender diversity, transpeople were recognized as being especially gifted at building bridges between the seen and the unseen, time and eternity. The great Puritan poet John Milton wrote in *Paradise Lost* that the angels of God are gender-fluid shape-shifters, who can 'either sex assume, *or both*' – and that these transgender angels can make love with one another as trans-angels whenever they so desire (*Paradise Lost* I. 423–31). The Sumerian goddess Inanna transcended gender polarities and sometimes turned men into women or women into men. Many of her priests and the priests of Cybele were eunuchs or transwomen. To this day many African tribes have religious leaders who are transpeople. Burmese *acault* are known for their cross-gender behaviours and are highly regarded as servants of a female spirit. Many shamanic traditions honour transpeople as well as same-sex lovers for their expert spiritual facilitation. I refer interested readers to Leslie Feinberg's *Transgender Warriors* (1996) and my own book *Omnigender* (2001) for further details about transgender people as bridges or gate-keepers to deeper, more fully spirited states of being. Perhaps this gift has been nurtured in us by our struggles to unify the various aspects of our inner natures. Whatever: it seems to me that if contemporary religious congregations are eager to develop a more mature spirituality, they will seek out the considerable spiritual gifts of the transpeople in their midst.

Fifth, by the circumstances of our lives we transpeople have been forced to do a lot of introspection about sex, gender, justice and spirituality. Yet we live in a society that is really quite divided and distraught concerning gender/sexuality's connections to justice and spirituality. Christian churches especially have fallen into such fear of embodiment and sexual pleasure that they are spending inordinate amounts of time on issues like same-sex marriage, contraception and abortion, meanwhile sometimes ignoring the facts that 1.3 billion people are starving, that global warming is catastrophic, that huge military budgets are killing the world's economies and that health-care needs are unmet for millions of people. Many congregations in the USA are still supporting the expenditure of millions of dollars on sex-education that urges teenagers to pledge celibacy until marriage – ignoring the mounting evidence that teens who have taken virginity pledges are four times more likely to have oral sex and six times more likely to have anal sex than those who refused to take the pledge (Haffner 2008, p. 101).

It has always interested me that when the author of Ephesians wanted to depict marital love, he did so by imagery of Christ and the Church, urging that every Christian (male or female) should defer to every other Christian out of reverence for Christ, the anointed child of God (Eph. 5.1). The public or communal nature of this imagery seems to me to indicate that passionate love for one other individual should open up our hearts to loving people in general, so that, if our love is genuine love, there is no way that it can rightfully exclude others from its embrace.

I certainly do not take this to mean that we must behave sexually with everyone we love, but instead this: that if what we call love causes us to hunker down and care about nobody beyond our immediate partner and family we need to take a more critical look at what we are designating as *love*.

Thoughtful readers may by now be wondering why I should think that transpeople are particularly well suited to teach congregations about the multiple and profound connections between sex, gender, love and justice. Well, for one reason, because we know how 'outsider' status feels, and many of us are mature enough to want to spare others from the hurt we have endured. For another, because we have had to *study* gender and sex and how to achieve justice in a way that sex-and-gender-normative people have never been forced to do. For yet another, we have a great transgender role model in Jesus of Nazareth, who was a very androgynous human being. Even if Jesus was not intersexual chromosomally (a possibility I mentioned earlier) he was still androgynous because he transgressed so many of the gender/sexual rules of his place, time and culture, including the failure to marry, the doing of 'women's work' such as cooking and washing feet, the willingness to associate himself with the female personification of God's Wisdom, and the willingness to apply birthing, breast-feeding and other female metaphors to his descriptions of his work on this planet.

If we take seriously the New Testament descriptions of Jesus' relationships with Mary Magdalene and with the Beloved Disciple (John? Lazarus?), we might conclude that Jesus was bisexually oriented; and if so, it seems hugely ironic that, in our society, bisexuals are still forced into invisibility and powerlessness, often out of loyalty to a Jesus who was perhaps one of them. It is also ironic that people who cannot or will not obey our society's inaccurate and unjust binary gender norms should be persecuted in the name of Jesus, who was possibly intersexual but certainly a gender transgressor in many other ways. It is also ironic that right-wing Christians should oppose same-sex marriage in the name of Jesus and 'family values', when in fact Jesus exalted the love of friends, *not* marital love, as the greatest love there is (John 15.11–13), and had many negative things to say about putting the love of family above the love of God and like-minded companions.

Amy-Jill Levine, an orthodox Jew and New Testament scholar at Vanderbilt University, says that Jesus' anti-family comments would have made him quite unpopular among the Jews of his place and time (Levine 2006, pp. 55–6). Yet today many congregations turn a deaf ear to Jesus' critique of 'family values'. It falls therefore to transpeople and our allies to lift up Jesus' understanding of love as mutual concern, deference and compassion, the kind of fair-minded egalitarian love that good friends feel for one another.

I was recently shocked to learn that some right-wing Evangelicals are now teaching that the Christian Trinity is not co-equal, but that Jesus is in fact subordinate to the Father, and the Holy Spirit is subordinate to both the Father and the Son. Why, I asked myself, is this flirtation with the Arian heresy surfacing now, for the first time in public since the fourth century CE? The answer: subordinationism is being used to preserve male supremacy in the home and church. If any readers find this as astonishing as I do, they might want to check out the report from the Religion News Service. I saw it in *The Christian Century* (20 February 2007) in a news article entitled 'In Gender Debate, Jesus is Subordinate'. This development only highlights the wisdom of Jesus in exalting the love of friends rather than marital love, since for centuries marriage has been structured around the concept of male primacy and female secondariness. Will Roscoe was right on target when he wrote, 'In place of stratified social relations, Jesus holds up the comradely ideal of love. This way of loving suspends existing hierarchies and transforms unequal relationships into egalitarian ones' (Roscoe 2004, p. 75). Truly, religious congregations need the transgender presence as witness to the intimate connections between gender, sexuality, spirituality and human justice.

Sixth, because we transpeople embody 'the forgotten middle ground' or ambiguity itself, we can help to heal religious addictions to certainty. Left unchecked, the conviction that the world is divided into good and evil empires, with our nation and our religion everything that is good, yet confronted by evil all around – left unchecked, that addiction to dualistic certainty will destroy our entire planet. At this time, conditions in the world are so dangerous, so charged with 'us-versus-them' religious bitterness and ethnic warfare, that we might be forgiven for assuming that things are hopeless. But as historians like Karen Armstrong have shown us, the great religious and philosophic traditions that have nourished human hope for centuries *all* had their inception during the period from the ninth to the second centuries BCE. And these were centuries of hideous violence!

Space does not permit me to describe the many horrors that Karen Armstrong sets forth in her book *The Great Transformation* (2006). I urge you to read that book for yourself if you would like to kindle in yourself the hope that indeed, 'the darkest hour is just before dawn'. Armstrong shows that from the ninth to the second century BCE, Confuciansim and Taoism developed in China, Hinduism and Buddhism developed in India; monotheism developed in Israel, and philosophic rationalism developed in Greece. And out of the monotheism of Israel flowered three other major traditions: Rabbinic Judaism, Christianity and Islam.

What do every one of these traditions have in common? All of them emphasize, in one way or another, the abandonment of egocentricity in favour of a spirituality centred in lovingkindness and compassion. Each of the sages responded to the violence of each place and time by calling for self-criticism and the shouldering of personal responsibility. And each insisted that insight must be followed by practical and effective action. Human beings have never surpassed these teachings. Yet in our own time, we seem to be turning religion into something opposite to those teachings. Instead of viewing religion as something that humanizes our behaviour at a profound level, many of our contemporaries are willing to fight battles over doctrines or metaphysics, over belief systems, over knowledge that will eventually vanish away.

Armstrong points out that to the sages of all the great religions, religion *is* compassion: 'First you must commit yourself to the ethical life, then disciplined and habitual benevolence, not metaphysical conviction, would give you intimations of the transcendence you sought' (Armstrong 2006, p. xiv). Never until recently was it an orthodox belief system that constituted religion; it was 'respect for the sacred rights of all beings'. What all the sages have always known is that 'sympathy cannot be confined to our own group . . . we must all learn to "yield" to one another' (Armstrong 2006, p. 398). Remember: 'Each tradition developed in societies like our own that were torn apart by violence and warfare as never before; indeed, the first catalyst for religious change was usually a principled rejection of the aggression that the sages had witnessed all around them' (Armstrong 2006, p. xiv).

Our catalysts are events like the Holocaust, Bosnia, the disasters of 9/11, Iraq, Darfur, college and school killings and the like. Transpeople know what it is like to be in the middle, both male and female perhaps, neither male nor female perhaps, often rendered invisible or judged as evil by the dominant paradigms of our place and time. We also know that we are well-meaning but not always 'good'; we know that we are a mixture of 'good' and 'evil' just as everyone else is. So our experience of both-and, of being the often-forgotten middle of the gender continuum, makes us ideal for teaching our fellow-congregants the deceptively simple, deceptively difficult message central to all true religion: 'Love thy neighbour as thyself.'

Of course the love taught by the sages does not refer exclusively to sexual love, but neither does it exclude sexual love. Eros – our sexual drive – is a spiritual urge, driving us toward connectedness. It can be misused, and *is* misused, any time we use sex to gain control or dominance over others. But our *eros* can also 'inspirit' and inspire us to reach out in compassion toward others.

I was moved to read in Cris Beam's book *Transparent* (2008) about a group of teenage transpeople in Los Angeles who mentor and assist one another in learning the skills necessary for survival in a transgender-phobic society. Who taught these trans-teenagers to be so helpful and faithful to one another? Chris Beam found that:

> whether they're still being parented at home or not, many transgender teenagers will find new parents. These parents are called drag mothers or drag fathers, and often they are just a few years older than their 'children' . . . They'll mentor anywhere from a handful to dozens of the younger street kids, sometimes renting out large apartments as shelter for the more transitory kids. This especially happens in Harlem . . . (Beam 2008, p. 55)

Instead of allowing their own suffering to make them bitter, these drag mothers and fathers somehow find it possible to transform their pain into supportiveness for those growing up after them. I think many religious congregations might need to learn about love and 'keeping faith' from transpeople of this compassionate type!

Seventh, and finally, transfolk are valuable to religious congregations because, with all our diversities, we incarnate the truth that just as all races are 'one blood', all genders and sexualities are 'one continuum' – and also that the 'one blood' and 'one continuum' is sacred, holy, divine. When he was speaking to the Athenian philosophers on Mars Hill, the Apostle Paul not only quoted the transgender Epimenides to the effect that 'in [God] we live, and move, and have our being' (Acts 17.28) but also said that God had 'made of one blood all nations [of humankind] to dwell on all the face of the earth' (Acts 17.26). What mincemeat Paul's statement makes of the old racist rule that if a person's bloodstream contained even one drop of 'black blood' the person's race must be Black, as opposed to the normative and privileged White race with 100 per cent Caucasian blood! Thanks to DNA studies, we now know that many so-called Black people have 30 per cent or more of Caucasian or 'Euro' blood, while many so-called White people have 30 per cent or more of African blood. And we now know that all of the atoms in our bodies are replaced every seven years, moving into other bodies or into the atmosphere. So the atoms that make up the bodies of all persons are identical and constantly interchanging as our tissues age and die and rebuild. Indeed, 'God made of one blood all nations to dwell on all the face of the earth'! And if religious people had believed and acted upon their own sacred texts, they would never have indulged in slavery or other forms of racism, and nobody would be attacking anybody else for being located differently on a sex-gender continuum that is in constant flux anyway.

If we could line up the entire human race from darkest skin to lightest skin, where would 'Black' end? Where would 'White' begin? And if we could line up the entire human race from most male to most female, where would 'masculinity' end and 'femininity' begin, and what would those concepts mean in the first place? If indeed every one of us lives in God and has our being within the divine womb, what difference does it make if we have relatively minor, benign diversities?

All diversities point toward one great Spirit who chose to incarnate in millions of different forms. As the Hebrew prophet Jeremiah put it, 'Do I not fill heaven and earth? says the Lord' (Jer. 23.24) – which means that there is *no space left in the universe* for anything or anyone that is not sacred. Similarly, the apostle Paul wrote to the Corinthians, 'There are varieties of activities, but it is the same God who activates all of them in everyone' (1 Cor. 12.6). And the Psalmist exclaimed, 'Where can I go from your spirit? Or where can I flee from your presence?' (Ps. 139.7), concluding that the holy one is indeed everywhere. Sufi mystics as well as biblical wisdom tell us that each person is an unknown name of God. Personally, I do not want to run the risk of mistreating or excluding any person in whom some aspect of God's mystery might be revealed to me.

I conclude this essay with some questions for those readers who may or may not consider themselves gender-different, but who are pastors, priests, rabbis, imams, or otherwise leaders within their various religious congregations. Does it matter to you that the Bible honours transpeople? Could your congregation use some help in rising above harmful stereotypes of what 'real men' and 'real women' are supposed to be? Could your congregation's pronouns and images concerning God be more supportive of human justice by becoming more diverse? Could you use some congregants who are especially gifted at bridging the gap between time and eternity, the seen and the unseen? Could your congregation be making healthier connections between sexuality, gender, spirituality and human justice? Could some of your congregants use some assistance in transcending their addictions to certainty, their 'pelvic orthodoxy' as well as their 'us-versus-them' categorizations of 'good' and 'evil'? Could your congregation profit from additional inhouse examples of the fact that we live in a divine milieu, where everyone and everything has its being within God's being? If your heart has answered yes to any of these questions, then you have acknowledged that your congregation needs to seek out the gifts of its transgender members – and needs to invite more transpeople to enter into your fellowship.

References

'Mixed Messages', *The Advocate* (8 April 2008), pp. 29–33.

Armstrong, Karen (2006), *The Great Transformation: The World in the Time of Buddha, Socrates, Confucius and Jeremiah* (New York: Atlantic Books).

Beam, Cris (2008), *Transparent: Love, Family, and Living the T with Transgender Teenagers* (Philadelphia: Harvest Books).

Carden, Michael (2006), 'Genesis/Bereshit', in Deryn Guest, Robert E. Goss, Mona West and Thomas Bohache, eds, *The Queer Bible Commentary* (London: SCM Press), pp. 21–60.

Daly, Mary (1973), *Beyond God the Father* (Boston: Beacon Press).

Feinberg, Leslie (1996), *Transgender Warriors* (Boston: Beacon Press).

Haffner, Debra N. (2008), *What Every 21st Century Parent Needs to Know* (New York: Newmarket Press).

Kessel, Edward I. (1983), 'A Proposed Biological Interpretation of the Virgin Birth', *Journal of the American Scientific Affliation* 35, pp. 129–36.

Levine, Amy-Jill (2006), *The Misunderstood Jew* (San Francisco: HarperSanFrancisco).

Mollenkott, Virginia R. (1983), *The Divine Feminine* (New York: Crossroad).

Mollenkott, Virginia R. (2001), *Omnigender: A Trans-religious Approach* (Cleveland, OH: Pilgrim Press).

Plaskow, Judith (2007), 'The Challenge of Transgender to Compulsory Heterosexuality', in Marvin M. Ellison and Judith Plaskow, eds, *Heterosexism in Contemporary World Religion* (Cleveland, OH: The Pilgrim Press), pp. 13–36.

Roscoe, Will (2004), *Jesus and the Shamanic Tradition of Same-Sex Love* (San Francisco: Suspect Thoughts Press).

4

Through the Wilderness

KRZYSZTOF BUJNOWSKI

I have lived in the same country all my life, and yet I have been a refugee within it for as long as I can remember. The epithet 'stranger in a strange land' is one I can identify with. I did my best to follow the rules but conformity was only skin deep. Underneath I struggled to find how I could experience the easy confidence of those who belonged.

I come from a family that has put a lot of effort into keeping up appearances. It secures social standing and that has been important for different reasons for both my parents, one of whom was indeed a refugee. They have needed to act in ways that are important to and recognized by society; even if those ways involve secrets and lies in the manufacture of appearance. My family is adept at separating out and discarding, where necessary, the truth in favour of something that seems more palatable. They are not bad people; on the contrary, they are like many others of their generation and position. My father, for example, liked to see himself as a pillar of his exiled community; he was a regular churchgoer, a dedicated member of many committees and a generous donor to charitable causes. My mother was more concerned with privacy; her devotion to the regard of her neighbours whether or not she knew them, indeed to a broader and unknowable public, became stronger with every encounter that shook her faith. She tried desperately to hand this regard on to me. It is a poisoned chalice, however, when truth suppressed corrodes one's life to the extent that it does not seem worth living.

The particular truth which my mother wished to remain hidden became a burden to me when I was young because I loved my mother and regarded her as the fount of all knowledge. She was my barometer on the world outside. What she thought, 'they' thought. So I kept my truth to myself: it was not acceptable to her and it would not be acceptable to anyone else.

I held the shame within me, allowing it to keep on wracking and wrecking mind and body. The truth that could not be told is that I am a man born into a woman's body. A man who, because he appeared to be a woman, was treated as a woman and who gave up an unequal fight to be recognized and, exhausted and close to despair, hid behind his appearance.

I am just an ordinary bloke who, for 50 years lived inside an extraordinary body. I inhabited the space within but was uncomfortable outside. This meant that I did not get on well with other bodies and people who inhabited them. Strange wording, strange idea: to separate bodies from people. Most people have no need to do that, they live joined-up lives and it would not occur to them to think in this tortuous way. It fascinates me how men and women have a basic confidence that emanates from a central certainty about who, no, about what they are.

This inner, unconscious certainty is projected into their behaviour and into their appearance. Because they are confident about it then they can afford to be off guard even in social encounters. I cannot think of a time when I have not been on guard, patrolling every nuance of behaviour in myself and others; alert to every covert look, every use of pronoun and every gendered remark. The nature of so many social encounters is governed by gender – this first, most obvious category. For those of us whose gender does not conform to the body we inhabit, every social encounter is a potential danger. The most casual of encounters are full of danger, which is why in public I am on high alert for whispered comment, pointed remark, second glance, unabashed stare. The temptation to hunch one's shoulders, keep one's eyes looking at the ground rises up unbidden. Preparation for flight kicks into place instinctively, readiness to fight follows reluctantly. Mental and physical exhaustion can overcome me just posting a letter. It is an intolerable state of tension to be in day in and day out. There is a huge cost to being in the closet, for however much one is close to invisibility there are some things that just give one away.

The sureness of those who have never felt they had to question their gender identity is a matter of envy to others. For many of us who are transpeople the incongruities have been there from the earliest age: we have always lived with complexity as well as concealment. Now that more of us are coming out of hiding we are talking up the complexity of gender. It is not our invention – as we move from a psychiatric model to a psychological one to an endocrinological one – that offsets the inventions of others: it is our experience. For some of us the journey towards our true selves is as important as our getting there.

As a child, I had no power nor had I any trust in my parents. And for those reasons, I never learned any strategies to outwit my parents. My time at a Catholic Girls Grammar School complete with Catholic morality upheld my parents' position. Gradually, I relied on a fantasy life to get me through, and to reduce the humiliation and despair I felt to a manageable level. In my daydreams I was always the hero; noble, courageous, faced with impossible odds and invariably tortured, subjected to trials and tribulations that I would eventually overcome. And I always rescued and got the girl. This phase of my life could be called 'Early Christian Martyr'.

These dreams kept me sane; but kept me battened down in my parents' world, in the social world. I relied on the dreams to get me through my days; I used them as substitutes for the life I wanted to lead and they were infinitely better than the life I did lead. They had another consequence though, they masked the need for me to come to terms with life how it is, so that I never learned any strategies that helped me deal with my life and helped me change it. I now read stories of transmen who, in their twenties and thirties go through their transition, often on their own, and I wonder however did they manage with such little support? I was still tied to my parents when I was 19 and even into my thirties and forties I gave my parents power over me. Even though I saw them very little for some years, still there was this desire to please; there was the unconscious censoring of my thoughts and wishes. I was almost paralysed by passivity in the face of a need to be approved by these two people. I spent most of my life trying to get them to love me as I am but it was always destined to fail. My mother disapproved of how I looked, what I did and who I was with. She passed on to me by her body language and, by her comments, that she was uncomfortable when I wanted to talk about myself. She slid away from confrontation; if she was hijacked she would start to cry. There was nothing I could do to get her to listen just to me. Somehow her disapproval, of what she was not always able to articulate, wrapped around her impenetrably. I see now that she was fearful.

When I was growing up, the term transsexuality was not in the common discourse nor was it easily found in popular psychological texts. The closest name I could find was homosexuality. I read what I could to find out why I was different, but all of the literature focused on male homosexuality. It referred to feminized men as a psychological phenomenon: they had an absent or ineffectual father and/or a dominant mother. The literature only cursorily mentioned women, these of course were all lesbians and the reason for their behaviour was glossed over, perhaps mooting the idea of a psychological rejection of 'normal' behaviour in society in favour of a closed, one-sex world. It usually mentioned dominant 'butch' lesbians and passive feminine women in relationships that were assumed to ape heterosexual married life. These people were a source of pity or disdain, depending on whether the text I was reading was written by a psychiatrist or a feminist. Whether or not these 'butch' women were transsexual men was not an issue back then; that they suffered from 'penis envy' was uppermost in the authors' minds. So the closest fit I had was to be a butch lesbian, who dressed and acted like a man, wanted to be a man but was definitely a woman with a problem.

My mother was very effective in her campaign to make me feel her disgust at behaviours described then as sexually deviant but which in reality challenged the binary gender divide. I internalized some of those feelings and reproduced them as my own. Whenever I saw very butch-looking women (who may be butch lesbians after all), I was extremely nervous that that was what people saw me as. I saw the covert looks people sent over and the hasty looks away should she or he look in their direction. I felt pity for their loneliness and vulnerability. Classic homo- and transphobia, I see now, with a bit of projection thrown in for good measure. The conviction I had that I was truly male was being eroded by everything and everyone around me.

I hate the idea of being looked at by strangers, pitied or repulsed: both I dislike. This no doubt goes back not only to my mother's reaction but also to when I was young and boyish looking, and thin enough to look androgynous. Strangers had no qualms in asking me whether I was a boy or a girl; calling me names; speculating on my reproductive capacity; talking about me loudly to their companions. Even when I was with others it did not prevent strangers from passing comment directly to me or to others. Of course, I became highly sensitized to it, embarrassed and mortified. For a long time it did not prevent me from dressing the way I wanted but eventually, having been rejected by my girlfriend who told me my feelings were a phase and I would grow out of it, I allowed my hair to grow long and straight. I could justify it to the real me because by this time we were in the late sixties and it was fashionable for men to have long hair. And I looked slightly more feminine to the ordinary punter in the street.

So I opted for disguise and deception. I already wore several masks. These varied from those I had to wear in my persona as a girl, for example, school uniform and other female clothes; to making sure my manner and gait, conversation and general demeanour in company were female enough to get by.

I have been told that I acquired emotional intelligence at an early age, when I was too young to know what to do with it. My physical world right away was dangerous and painful; there was nothing and no one I could trust. In early adolescence this 'intelligence' manifested itself in a political sophistication not often echoed by others, an empathy with 'the underdog'; courage and passion to try to right their wrongs and, paradoxically, a cynicism that was noticed when I was quite young – 12 – first named by one of my teachers. The flipside to this 'intelligence' was a bitterness and private anguish that occasionally manifested itself as anger, rudeness or withering comments. Later, after I had grown my hair long, the public comments changed from 'are you a boy or a girl?' to 'cheer up, it may never happen'. I have never quite got the hang of this arrogance and righteousness, whereby strangers have a right to make public judgements in the guise of passing comments.

My watchfulness increased as I grew older. In company I could never fully rest so I had to absorb the tension that was being created. At junior school I was regarded as very bright and intellectually mature. When I went to grammar school this reputation was enhanced but, as the toll of hiding went on, my schoolwork suffered. Not my class work. I remained one of the brightest there. But I found it difficult to do my homework. I would get out the exercise book and the text book and would sit, staring at them until I was called to do something else or until I could reasonably be held to have completed a piece of work. Mostly, during that time I was fantasizing, daydreaming about what I wanted life to be like; or I was struggling to understand what made me different and so unhappy. All of the time, I had no doubt that I was male. Some huge mistake had been made but I could not see how I could put it right. Until puberty hit me, there was always the hope that things would sort themselves out. After, there was no hope left. Depression and despair became constant companions and poisoned what was left of my resilience. I did not feel safe disclosing anything to my parents. I learned to lie by deflecting questions, giving evasive or cryptic answers, and if those tactics failed then I could always resort to anger. Revision was the worst time and as a result I scored fewer and fewer marks in exams. I could still come up with the occasional intriguing essay but mostly my head was so full of pain that I could not concentrate on schoolwork.

It is a cliché in the world of female-to-male transpeople that the onset of menstruation is the death knell of hope. And so it was. The signs I had looked out for – the deepening voice, the increase of facial hair – had all misled. They were false promises of what was to come. This was the beginning as far as I remember of the serious work to dissociate myself from my body.

It was inevitable that I began to hate myself. Whoever 'myself' was. I hated the self that was the body of a woman, the self that was viewed by everyone. I hated the self that made me disguise my body and opened the way for strangers and intimates alike to feel they could comment on my appearance. I had another self, the hurt, crying self that wanted to curl up and sleep away through life so that I need not disappoint it and it could not hurt me further.

Maybe if I had broken down completely, not adjusted my behaviours to manage and to keep in control, then maybe the professionals could have stepped in sooner and offered me a way through. But this was the 1960s and I was more likely to be given electroconvulsive therapy (ECT) than hormones or chest surgery. So hiding was probably the safe thing to do. But hiding by trying to pass as a boy and a man was impossible: a dilemma throughout my adult life was that my body just could not 'pass' without first having chest surgery – I was too big.

I discovered that I had to prove that not living outwardly as a man was causing me psychological damage. I was loath to be diagnosed as mad. Mad meant hospital; mad meant doped beyond consciousness; mad meant electric shocks; mad meant loss of control. In any case, if I were mad, then surgery would be denied me. At the same time, I was outwardly handling my dilemma well; how could I be diagnosed as being psychologically damaged? I was stuck in an unyielding logic. If only I were able to let go, if only I were able to trust enough to have a breakdown, then I might have had help sooner.

Puberty was a great watershed; after it I could no longer trust my body to look how I wanted it to look. It was no longer easy to appear androgynous, so I had to make compromises with my clothing. *Why* was it that I took the decision to hide, back in the teenage years, rather than make the decision to escape and seek to authenticate my self? Perhaps I was desperate to gain my parents' approval and so I subsumed my authentic self as best I could in order to gain acceptance.

Where was God in all this? Didn't I seek refuge in prayer? Well, yes, I tried very hard. The Catholic primary school I attended was run by nuns; the church was next door; the priest was a frequent visitor. By the age of nine, I was almost fervent. I said my daily prayers; I went to confession every three weeks; to Mass every week and I took Holy Communion with all the humility I could muster. On Sunday afternoons, I was given to playing 'Mass' with myself as the priest (the only time I would willingly wear a dress was on these Sunday afternoons when I would appropriate a particular dress of my mother's that resembled a cassock when worn by a nine year old) and my brother played the altar boy. I even considered whether or not I had a vocation. But this is where reality kicked in, because I could see myself as a priest, indeed I was seriously drawn to life as a Franciscan monk; but the only position I would be considered for would be that of a nun. Vocation over.

As I grew from child to young person to adult I saw doors closing not opening. So many things depend on gender as a passport for inclusion. So it was with religion. It was also clear to me that I was a sinner and that the sin was so unacceptable it could never be voiced, not even, not especially, in the confessional. Yet there was no hiding place, for Catholics can sin in thought as well as word and deed. So even my fantasy life was forbidden; even the mental struggle I was having trying to understand myself was an act of sin. There was no respite.

Yet, I argued to myself, this is the Church's thinking; God and especially Christ were kinder than that. I could not believe that the Christ of the New Testament who empathized with thieves and prostitutes would deny me my thoughts. It was this above all else that turned me away from religion. I started to see religions as power organizations, social groups as any other that inevitably could not cope with difference. The power exerted to make one conform was for me counter-productive. In the end I could moderate my behaviour to appear to conform but that bore no relation to my truth. The Church could have my body but not my soul. Religion over.

I continued to pray in those bleak moments when playing sport or dwelling within my thoughts were not enough. I spent several years looking for God, needing, like Thomas, a visible sign of his godliness. I never found it. On the contrary, I came to believe in nothing but the possibility of humanity. For all my professed cynicism, I was above all else moved by the plight of others. Misunderstood by my parents, rejected by the girl I loved, by the time I was 15 I never thought I could find anyone to love me; and suicide was a serious option. On a school outing to a junior school for children with special needs I was approached by a young girl who took my hand and would not let go. On leaving, I realized that I, just as much as she, did not want to let go. I felt immense sympathy for her: her future world was not going to be easy to live in. I felt an immense gratitude to her for offering me the simple gift of touch. I felt an immense loneliness as we said goodbye. It felt like a betrayal for me to pull my hand away. I wanted to take care of her, to protect her from the alien and unwelcoming world, yet I also knew that was fulfilling a need in me. I knew the urge was not noble and selfless as one likes to think charitable acts and thoughts can be; and I loathed myself for my selfishness.

That event though was the beginning of my salvation. It was not a damascene moment but it heralded a new layer in my understanding. The god that I had been taught about could not, did not, exist. I could find him nowhere. I could find no evidence and I had no faith. But people who were less fortunate than me were everywhere. My instinctive empathy could be turned to good use, as long as I could curb my own neediness. And that, as it turned out was relatively easy; I simply had to fill my life with activity. So, even before I left school I had perfected a way to hide who I was and, as a volunteer worker, I entered the underworld of people who slept on the streets, in shelters, hostels and communities.

I was cradled by the Cyrenian community for some years though I believe I gave back as much if not more than I received. The empathy I held for those who had been pretty well rejected by everyone else enabled me to communicate with many and befriend some; I was able to give them shelter and food but also the non-judgemental acceptance that was so important; we were based after all on the man who had shouldered Christ's cross on the way to his death on Calvary: Simon of Cyrene. I embraced the romance of this while rejecting the religion. This life is a way of surviving in this world rather than a rehearsal for the next. If we are all we have then we have to have faith in each other and I might as well set an example. I say this with hindsight. At the time it was enough to know that life for some was even shittier than for me, yet they persisted in living and I began to realize how strongly we are tethered to life. My time with the Cyrenians helped me see that I was not a victim, that mentally I was quite tough and that for all my loneliness I was desperate to connect with people.

I embraced the concept of non-judgemental acceptance that was central to the Cyrenian philosophy. It was what I wanted for myself – for others not to judge me but to accept the person I am – so I had to offer it to others. It is hard work and I often fail but it is my own contribution to the planet. It is my step into faith together with a belief in reciprocity. It has to be a belief because it has often been disproved. My cynical self thinks what I am writing is romantic but untrue; there is so much evidence of the callous behaviour of so many I am right to fear what people can do. Yet some other part of my brain mutters that I do actually believe, if not in the goodness of people then in their potential for goodness, and this is enough.

It follows that I cannot reject those people who hold strong faith in their god or who are searching as I had done for safety and a place to belong. I do question whether the strong views which allow people of religion to reject their fellows on grounds of difference are the product of any deity. I know that to define a group by those outside it is an age-old measure of belonging. I have spent a number of years of my adult life studying the nature of men and women in groups: the need for belonging is strong in most of us, the need for survival is greater. Atrocities in the name of one religion or another are committed not only by the cynical or the psychopathic but by neighbour on neighbour.

Thirty years on from the Cyrenians I finally transitioned. I picked my moment, for times have changed; the state now promotes 'equality and diversity' and has legislated for the official recognition of transgendered people. My belief in people has borne fruit for I found a person who supported, encouraged and smoothed my path towards transition; and many others have been supportive and kind through my transition.

I am lucky. I survived despair and depression and ultimately became strong enough to stand up to my own transphobia and self-dislike. It did not happen because I had any sense of spirituality. I had dismissed religions, given up my search for a supreme being and realized I am truly an atheist. I live without God, so do I live without spirituality as well? I have no sense of anything connecting me to anything else apart from my fellowship with human beings, some of whom would hate the thought of a connection to people such as me. Others, though, love me and try to love me for what I am even if that is alien to them. Some have loved me enough to help set me free even at a great cost to themselves. It is they in whom I believe, and people like them who overcome their own fears to help others gain dignity and respect. So although I have no god, ultimately I have a faith which is enough to lock me into life on earth.

I have described the moral code I try to live by but this is underpinned by mundanity. I have no sense of the numinous in relation to humanity. The closest I come to a spiritual essence is when my body feels fully engaged with my mind. I get this when I am physically tested to the utmost. It is a memory now when I played volleyball to such a degree that was Zen-like or when I ran until I reached a zone beyond pain, or when I walked up mountains. The memories are precious, for these events happened before my transition and they were times when I had respite from otherwise continual mental pain. My physical health will not now allow me to play sport so my alternative is to reach out to the physical world. Even better when I can walk some way into the wilderness and become enraptured and awed by the natural world. When my soul is in darkness, and even when it is not, I lift my eyes to the hills. This for me is a respite from the hard work of social interaction; I do not know if it deserves the term spiritual; it seems too trite. Now that my mind and body are in conjunction perhaps the search for my spiritual world is my next mission.

5

Shot from both Sides: Theology and the Woman Who Isn't Quite What She Seems

SIÂN TAYLDER

Love the sinner, hate the sin

How many times have those of us lurking on the periphery of orthodox theologies heard that apparently innocuous little cliché being aimed in our general direction? Sounds reasonable enough, in the greater scheme of things, at least; *love the sinner, hate the sin* seems to encapsulate the concepts of forgiveness and redemption that form the tenets of Christ's teaching and eradicates, within one simple sentence, the more odious, misogynist and blatantly barmy decrees laid out in the Old Testament. It makes perfect sense, in theory at least, and can even lead us to a greater understanding of the nature of sin and how and why people commit crimes and injustices that might seem, on the surface at least, so inherently and incomprehensively wrong, if not downright evil. Those Catholics of a certain vintage (myself included) might even call upon it when analysing the nature of structural and personal sin that was central to the debates surrounding liberation theology in the sixties and seventies. Thus, when my rucksack gets slashed in the market in downtown San Salvador I don't blame the kid who did it, rather the socio-political systems that force him to engage in such acts.

That's all very well when it's nothing more valuable than ten dollars and a cheap camera that gets nicked: when it's your passport, travellers cheques and all your worldly goods, trite, liberal platitudes can wear a bit thin. At some point down the line, *love the sinner, hate the sin* descends into a debate about moral relativism. Back in the comfort of my safe European home, I can probably bring myself to forgive – assuming that's what the *love* in *love the sinner* essentially means – the ten-year-old Salvadoran urchin who stole my backpack, and even hope he's invested his proceeds well. What's not so easy is to bring oneself to *love* those who carry out abominable acts against ourselves and those we are immensely fond of. I speak from experience, not of having my backpack spirited away but of having been on the receiving end of a sin – a crime – so repulsive and life changing that I could never, ever bring myself to forgive.

Love the sinner, hate the sin. There is, of course, no sliding scale: if you forgive the pilfering child you have to forgive the calculating rapist. But where does that leave the likes of me? What if our 'sin' is not one of theft or violation but of daring to be different, a sin not of 'doing' but simply of 'being'. That's when *love the sinner, hate the sin* ceases to be a Christian mantra and becomes, instead, a diktat of theological orthodoxy, a stick with which to beat those who refuse to toe the line. *Love the sinner, hate the sin;* sounds like an exercise in Christian toleration when it is, of course, anything but.

Let me explain. I am writing this chapter in one of the smarter suburbs of San Salvador, the almost eponymous capital city of the Central American republic of El Salvador, which during the 1980s became synonymous with violence, injustice and, of course, liberation theology. It's only a 15-minute walk to the Catholic University of Central America (*La UCA*) where, on 16 November 1989, six Jesuit priests, their housekeeper and her daughter were murdered by one of the military's 'elite' death squads. *Love the sinner, hate the sin*? Not easy, is it? Not even from a liberal or radical perspective. We're already asking ourselves: which was the greater sin? Killing the priests or killing the young child?

A couple of weeks ago I was offered a teaching position at one of the country's more prestigious private schools, an institution so intensely and traditionally Catholic that the casual visitor could be forgiven for thinking she'd entered a nunnery. A college so conformist that even the teachers wear uniforms. None of which particularly fazed me given that I am, myself, a practising Catholic with a strong devotion to the Virgin of

Guadalupe (I've got the t-shirt, I've got the towel, all I need now are the crotchless knickers!).

For perfectly laudable reasons, foreign nationals are prohibited from taking up employment in El Salvador unless there's a specific need, and native English teachers are generally granted exemptions. Nevertheless, acquiring legal status involves a long and costly process requiring testimonies of conduct and the presentation of various documents, including birth certificates. Now, the educational establishment to which I refer enjoys close contact with the right-wing Salvadoran government and can be relied upon to procure legal status with a minimum of fuss and financial outlay. Having been offered the job and having agreed to start work the following day, I thought it only fair to mention that they would find certain discrepancies between the information given on my birth certificate and the information shown in my passport. The former alleged that I was born Simon Taylder and born a male; the latter quite clearly stated that I was Siân Taylder and a female. It shouldn't take a genius to work out what happened in between.

Love the sinner, hate the sin. The Principal continued smiling sweetly as she explained that the position was no longer available because my personal circumstances were not compatible with the ethos of the school – or words to that effect.

That one of El Salvador's most prestigious private schools chooses to discriminate against the likes of me doesn't unduly concern me because I, in turn, practise a rigid system of discrimination against those who subscribe to racist, homophobic (*transphobic*?) or sexist points of view; it's a theology of *quid pro quo*, and I don't see why I should be expected to tolerate those who refuse to tolerate me. What I did find grossly offensive was the clear insinuation that having the temerity to alter one's gender both superficially and surgically was considered a sin and that, in the eyes of the Catholic hierarchy, I was right down there with paedophiles, rapists and other, assorted sexually deviant malcontents; the assumption being that homosexuals – and thus, by definition, transsexuals are by their very natures child abusers and sex-offenders. It didn't so much hurt as fill me with anger, but do you know what? Two days later I went to Sunday mass at the church adjacent to the school and looked them all in the eye as I went up to receive communion: it was one way of meeting fire with fire.

That, to me, is the essence of Queer Theology, what makes it substantially different to other theologies of liberation, what makes it a potent force, what makes it dangerously – but playfully – subversive. It's like doing theology without underwear, like going to mass without your knickers on, like saying the rosary with a vibrator in your handbag because it creates a gloriously inappropriate clash of the decent and the indecent. I sometimes worry that the liberation theologies we've come to know and love aren't a little too tolerant, a little too passive and a little bit too self-reverential. I prefer a theology that's prepared to look its enemies in the eye and laugh at their sheer absurdity rather than give them any intellectual or academic credibility (Campbell 2006). I prefer a theology that's prepared to give its opponents a good kick in the teeth – metaphorically speaking of course – because you know what? I'm tired of having to play the victim.

You don't agree? You think my theology's a little too aggressive? Allow me, then, to give you an example of the kind of people we are up against – and by 'we' I include all sexual dissidents whatever their gender or sexuality.

As a transsexual/transgendered woman I include, high up on the list of those I love to dislike – oh, alright then, those I love to hate – the Evangelical Alliance, an unholy coalition of fundamentalist and conservative Christians whose sole purpose, it seems, is to fire off press releases against anyone and anything that contravenes their myopic – some, such as myself, would also say perverse and bigoted – interpretation of the Christian faith. You know what they say, 'if they had brains they'd be dangerous'; the Evangelical Alliance has long since had its knives out for transsexuals, and regularly floods the media with statements fulminating against what it clearly sees as an abomination before God. *Love the sinner, hate the sin*? No chance: 'Living an overtly transsexual life is not compatible with a Christian life' (Southam 2001).

In 2001, the Evangelical Alliance published a report demanding that gender-reassignment surgery be made illegal on the grounds that it was 'a fantasy and an illusion' and called for transsexuals to 'reorient their lifestyle in accordance with biblical principles and orthodox church teaching' (Southam 2001). The report concluded that 'Authentic change from a person's given sex is not possible and an ongoing transsexual lifestyle is incompatible with God's will' (ibid.).

So what would they have us do?

> We suggest that radical surgery, to manipulate their bodies into line with what they feel themselves to be, isn't right. We feel there is another solution. We would include prayer and psychological counselling in that. We don't accept that God makes mistakes. (Southam 2001)

I make light of the Evangelical Alliance and its Neanderthal – or should that be Old Testament – attitudes to transsexuality because, like the British National Party (BNP), they only have to open their mouths to reveal themselves as unreconstructed bigots. But, like the BNP, that does not render them utterly impotent; they might well be all mouth and no trousers but there are swathes of vulnerable people out there to whom they represent a real danger – spiritually, emotionally and, I'm afraid to say, physically. The Evangelical Alliance report commends the work of Parakaleo, 'a Christian ministry seeking to uphold Biblical values to the transvestite, transsexual and transgendered person'[1] that claims that people can be healed of their transsexual condition.

The Parakaleo website contains a litany of sob stories detailing gender reassignments gone wrong that wouldn't look out of place in a Sunday tabloid, in terms of content and veracity. In a narrative whose style resembles a parody of pornographic fantasy, it cites the case of 'Mandy' who lived successfully as a female and then joined a particular congregation only to return to her birth sex as 'James' following a 'conversion experience'.

Once 'Mandy' has exposed herself to the pernicious influence of the pastor, the self-righteous platitudes come thick and fast and the end result is as predictable as it is untrue.

---

1 <http://www.parakaleo.co.uk/>

> Great was the rejoicing when a fine, be-suited young James walked to the front on the first Sunday of the year to be 'introduced' to the church. I could only feel a deep gratitude to God for His wonderful grace and transforming power. In what might seem to have been one of the most challenging of pastoral cases, I can honestly say it was a joy to act as spiritual 'midwife in training'. (<www.parakaleo.co.uk> 2009)

Not only that. Freed from the evils of transsexuality (which, in a Hollywood blockbuster, would surely be played by a surly, dark-skinned foreigner with an Arabic or Eastern European accent) our hero/heroine 'announced his engagement to a girl in the church and they have since married, but that's another story!' (ibid.).

It is indeed because it isn't actually true! It's now widely known that 'James' has become 'Mandy' again though the story is still available on the Parakaleo website. What does Horace say? You may drive out nature with a pitchfork, but she will always keep coming back.

But the fairy-tale ending reveals the sinister side of organizations such as the Evangelical Alliance and Parakaleo. *Love the sinner, hate the sin*? Perhaps we should sometimes be a little wary of the dictum. It's not enough that 'Mandy' sees the error of her ways and reverts to 'James'; he/she must also succumb to that ultimate bastion of masculinity, marriage. Clearly there is an ulterior motive in Parakaleo's so-called outreach, that of restoring the status quo in terms of gender, sex and sexuality. While it professes concern for the psychological well-being of those suffering from gender identity disorder (and inferring, quite erroneously, that the vast majority of post-operative transsexuals are desperately unhappy and would give their right arm to return to their original gender) the evangelical opposition to all forms of 'gender-bending' is, of course, based upon Old Testament Scripture which should set the alarm bells ringing already (see, for example, Gen. 1.27; and Deut. 22.5).

It doesn't really matter whether or not Mandy stayed Mandy or became James, or whether she was Mandy one day and James the next; there will always be those who cannot or will not fit into to the neat, polarized concept of gender that society prefers, even when it sanctions transsexuals. I am old enough to remember the consternation caused by Boy George back in the 1980s simply because there were those who weren't sure whether it was a he or a she though those very same people who condemned him laughed out loud at Lily Savage who was not only obviously a man in a frock but a cruel caricature to boot. That was something I, too, discovered, at fancy dress parties during my student days – also the 1980s. Since time immemorial men have enjoyed dressing in women's clothes and, to a certain extent, creating caricatures and lampooning the sex that the vast majority of them professed to love.

That's when I realized I was different:

> That was the night when the isolation began, when it suddenly became clear that he was not like them at all, that he might have more in common with members of what he'd previously taken to be the opposite sex. He slipped out of the door, into the dark but very public and all-seeing night air. He felt alive, so very fucking alive and so very dangerously beautiful. He watched others watching him, looked hard for unwanted reactions but he was getting away with it. For the first time in his short life, Simon Taylder was slipping away, metamorphosing into something and someone else but I wasn't yet there to fill the void. (Taylder 2008)

And that's why the likes of the Evangelical Alliance and Parakaleo are so abhorred by the likes of me, those who take their conviction to its logical extremes. In the world of orthodox theology, the default gender is still male and the default sexuality still masculine and heterosexual; the liberal Protestant churches might have ordained women clergy but the androcentric hierarchy of power remains virtually unscathed and almost entirely intact. Small wonder, then, that the transsexual – especially the male-to-female transsexual – attracts so much contempt: they are the ultimate gender traitors. Remember what it says in Deuteronomy 23.1? 'He whose testicles are crushed or whose male member is cut off shall not enter the assembly of the Lord.' Well, that rules me out then.

Does it? Hell. Technically not. Without going into detail gender reassignment is as much about *conversion* as it is about *castratio*. In the end, it all comes down to a question of attitude but in queer theology the transsexual with an axe to grind can be a dangerous subversive. Not only do we forsake our masculinity, we turn conventional concepts of sexuality on their heads; never has sedition been so perfidiously seductive. No one likes us, we don't care.

Indeed, there are times when we actually prefer it that way. I have to confess that having the massed ranks of conservative, evangelical Christians ranged against me fills me with a sense of well-being; I must be doing something right. The best form of defence is attack and I take great pleasure in attracting their opprobrium: the more they revile and condemn the likes of me the more I congratulate myself for taking the correct course of action.

I don't know when or why the Catholic Church felt the need to throw its lot in with the evangelicals and engage in the debate over 'gender reassignment'. Given its position on reproductive rights, same-sex relationships and the role of women in general one might have thought it unequivocal and clear, but the reality is that the laity and much of the clergy have a healthy disregard for Vatican edicts to the extent that they will tolerate – or turn a blind eye to – practices and lifestyles expressly condemned by the Magisterium. Whether or not my own experience bears this out is a matter of conjecture; the more extensive research required to determine that is sadly absent but I can at least offer some personal observations and anecdotes on what it is to be both Catholic and transsexual and, on the other side of the coin, what it is to be transsexual and a feminist theologian. There are many who would say that neither position is tenable and that's when theology gets personal.

For as long as I can remember the Catholic Church remained conspicuously silent on the thorny but esoteric subject of transsexuality. While it continued to pontificate on other matters pertaining to sex, gender and sexuality – abortion, contraception, homosexuality – it remained steadfastly tight-lipped on the morality of the sex-change process. Perhaps they didn't think it worth pontificating about: if so, they were probably right. Perhaps they didn't know what they were talking about – nothing new there then. If I'd known then what I know now would I have persisted in rekindling my love affair with the Church? But of course I would, it's my church, my Virgin Mary, my *Salve Regina* as much as it is theirs.

While the evangelical/fundamentalist objections to medical intervention and surgery for transsexuals are based on Old Testament Scripture and its prescription of what it means to be male and female, that of Catholicism tends towards the 'natural law' tradition that has played such a significant role in its theology – both of which, it might well be argued, are essentially one and the same thing. Gender re-assignment is said to subvert the 'natural' order of male and female, and a church that is so strongly opposed to artificial birth control is hardly likely to condone the self-castration or loss of fertility it entails.

Let's not forget that fear and loathing of sex and sexuality – more specifically, female sexuality – underlines Catholic sexual morality and, while there is certainly a greater affirmation of the value of sexual pleasure among heterosexual married people in contemporary Catholic teaching, the Church continues to prescribe only vaginal-penile intercourse. Only conjugal coitus can be good; every other sexual activity is either 'foreplay' or perverse.

Historically, female physiology has never been taken seriously in the formation of the Catholic moral tradition wherein human sexuality was described overwhelmingly from the male perspective with an attitude overwhelmingly negative towards, as well as ignorant of, female sexuality. Whereas in the male experience orgasm and ejaculation are more or less synonymous, it was argued that for all humans the capacity for sexual pleasure was closely tied to a reproductive activity. Despite the fact that the clitoris, unlike the penis, has one function only – exquisite female sexual pleasure – and has no procreative purpose, the sexual experience is still described as a male norm.

So where does the transsexual fit into this arcane and convoluted conundrum? Having undergone a process which, to all extents and purposes, is considered a selfish act of self-mutilation am I condemned to purgatory before I've even passed away? Is it a vagina or isn't it? Is it a clitoris or not? Does it really matter? Not for the first time do we find ourselves stuck fast between a rock and a hard place. No place to go, no place to hide, no place to call home. Perhaps that's no bad thing: a theology for the itinerant and the pariah – isn't that what queer theology's all about?

Pariah, yes, martyr, no. That way lies victimhood and self-oppression. When my therapist, called in to deal with post-traumatic stress disorder, suggested I might have a guilt complex I looked at her in complete surprise. Of course, I have, I told her. I'm the proud owner of a guilt complex. I'm a Catholic; it comes with the territory. Poor woman; she shook her head when she thought I wasn't looking but I already knew she didn't approve. Indeed, I don't think she approved of any religious affiliations at all but I'm sure Catholicism would have come pretty high up on her list of proscribed faiths.

Guilt, yes, self-sacrifice, no. The former I am exceptionally fond of, it's a tired cliché I've turned into a fine art; the latter I draw the line at, no matter how much it appeals to my innate masochist tendencies. Why ever not? Because that's what *they* want you to do; the road to eternal life is paved with pleasures the righteous have passed by. Well, they don't just 'pass by', they make a great show and dance of their acts of self-abnegation; the greater our suffering on earth, the greater our reward in the hereon after.

Reminds me of a campaign slogan run by Christian Aid: 'We believe in life before death'. I've a better way of putting it, more forceful and direct and probably a little too crude for the faint of heart: 'Pray for the dead but fight like hell for the living.' Contrary to popular opinion I didn't become a woman just to lie back and think of salvation, to become a passive, demure little maiden (à la Virgin Mary, I can hear some of you say) who wouldn't say boo to a goose let alone look a member of the opposite sex in the eye. If you'd have met the shy, retiring creature that was my previous incarnation you'd understand exactly what I mean; strange how a constant stream of hormones and a little surgical intervention should make all the difference but that's what it did. If God does indeed make mistakes, it's a good job we've got the NHS to correct them. What was it the Evangelical Alliance would have me do? Accept that 'it is a myth for people to think that they can bypass the Creator and attempt to control their own destiny, identity, or gender' and 'pray for normality' – whatever that is. Well, we know full well what their idea of 'normality' is.

Do you know what? I'm barely into middle age. I'm already getting tired of constantly being told what to do – or rather, what not to do. They've been on at me since I was eight years old: don't grow your hair long, don't shave your legs, don't put on any eyeliner, don't wear that dress, don't quit your job to take off for El Salvador. Small wonder I've become a rebel without a cause (some would say a rebel without a clue).

Forget the construction of the Virgin Mary as 'rich, white woman who does not walk' (Althaus-Reid 2004), or even as a rich, white who doesn't smoke, drink or swear or have an eye for the ladies; if you'll forgive the intentional irony, the Virgin Mary I've become devoted to has got balls, metaphorically if not literally – and in any case who knows exactly what's underneath that cloak. The Virgin Mary I've grown to love is not just Our Lady of Perpetual Succour or Our Lady of the Sorrows (though it's vitally important that she plays these roles, too), she's Nuestra Señora del Puño Cerrado – Our Lady of the Clenched Fist.

It was 2003 when the Vatican decided to throw its hat into the ring, suddenly declaring (and it came from out of nowhere) that 'sex-change' procedures do not change a person's gender in the eyes of the Church, adding that:

> The key point is that the (transsexual) surgical operation is so superficial and external that it does not change the personality. If the person was male, he remains male. If she was female, she remains female. (Norton 2003)

Furthermore:

> The altered condition of a member of the faithful under civil law does not change one's canonical condition, which is male or female as determined at the moment of birth. (Norton 2003)

The text goes on to define transsexuality as a

> psychic disorder of those whose genetic makeup and physical characteristics are unambiguously of one sex but who feel that they belong to the opposite sex. In some cases, the urge is so strong that the person undergoes a 'sex-change' operation to acquire the opposite sex's external sexual organs. (Norton 2003)

But it's the concluding phrase that gives the game away:

> The new organs have no reproductive function. (Norton 2003)

When I read that statement I didn't know whether to laugh or cry. Not because it effectively prevented me from entering into a valid marriage, rendered me liable to expulsion from a religious order (had I had the temerity to enter one) and curtailed any future career as a nun or priest ('unsuitable candidates for priesthood and religious life because of mental instability') although, interestingly, had they already been ordained a priest the latter 'can continue to exercise their ministry privately if it does not cause scandal' (Norton 2003). No, what upset me was that it went down the same road as the evangelicals in assuming that those suffering from gender dysphoria are of unsound mind and that the gender reassignment procedure 'increases the likelihood of depression and psychic disturbance' (Norton 2003). It was all the more bewildering because at the time I was a very active member of a Catholic congregation on the south coast of England. Whether or not my ill-fated and illicit personal history was widely known I never knew but I would like to think that most of my fellow parishioners (and what a nice, middle-class bunch they were) didn't give the proverbial two hoots.

You've got to admire the Catholic Church's ability to get round it's own Magisterium – to break it's own rules, whether it's for practical purposes (the priesthood is celibate, unless, of course, you're seeking refuge from the now female-dominated Church of England) or to prevent yet another public outrage (far too many examples to mention). But if you have to admire the Catholic Church's ability to get round its own Magisterium, you've got to admire all the more the ability of the laity to blatantly ignore it, even in the most unlikely of places. Even in fiercely faithful Mexico:

> MEXICO CITY, May 17 2008 – A couple who both changed their sex married on Saturday in Mexico's first transgender wedding, as the traditionally conservative country loses some of its inhibitions. Mario del Socorro, formerly Maria, and Diana Guerrero, who used to be

José, held an austere ceremony for friends and relatives in a community centre.

The couple said they hoped media coverage would pressure Mexico's Congress to pass a proposed law that would let people get sex change operations in public hospitals and then be able to change their names and genders in public records.

'When you are applying for a job and your documents don't coincide with what you look like, you just don't get hired. It's that simple,' said del Socorro, 55, who is balding with a wispy goatee and stands several inches shorter than his new bride.

Lawmakers behind the transgender proposal are challenging a swath of conservative customs in largely Catholic Mexico, and in recent years they have been gaining momentum.

In 2006, gay civil unions were legalized in Mexico City and the northern state of Coahuila. Lawmakers in the capital last year legalized early-term abortions and approved a law allowing terminally ill people to refuse treatment. The Catholic Church has strongly criticized all of these measures.

Del Socorro and Guerrero got married under their pre-sex change names because the law allowing gay civil unions does not give partners the same benefits as a traditional marriage.

At the ceremony, guests cheered the teary-eyed groom and beaming bride as they cut two tall wedding cakes before a crowd of journalists.

Members of the bride's Catholic family said the couple tried for months to find a priest that would marry them in a church.

'At the end of the day, it's a marriage between a woman and a man, so what's the problem with blessing this union in the eyes of God?' said the bride's sister. (Rosenberg 2008)

Shortly after the Vatican's 2003 pronouncements on the validity of the 'sex-change' procedure, the then assistant editor of *The Tablet* called me to solicit my opinion (which almost made me feel the acceptable face of Catholic transsexuality!). I said that I felt disappointed – but not surprised – that the Church had felt it necessary to enjoin battle against what the medical profession considered a valid and distressing condition. She also asked whether I would be changing the name and gender entered on my birth certificate, to which I replied no, I'd grown tired of tinkering with history and sometimes we have to live with unpalatable truths.

Would it, she wondered, force me to reconsider my position vis-à-vis the Catholic Church? I told her I'd been through that already – and look what good it did me.

I was born and raised a Catholic in the way that most English Catholics of the post-Vatican II era were (and for reasons I hope are quite clear I use the word 'English Catholicism' advisedly). Until the recent influx of Catholic migrants from Eastern Europe and elsewhere, a brief survey of the average congregation would have revealed a huge dent in the demographic; young people from their late teens to their mid-thirties were conspicuous by their absence and I was amongst that adolescent exodus. Not necessarily because I was bored – I've always been fascinated by religion – but because I virulently took against it. Given my loathing for what I considered to be an oppressively male institution, the manner in which I later returned is more than a little ironic.

I realized at a relatively young age that I wasn't going to grow up like other boys though it wasn't until the age of 21 that I realized I wasn't going to be a boy for much longer, and that I wasn't going to grow up to be a man. Here is not the place to go into the mechanics or the whys or wherefores. Suffice to say that I developed an intense dislike for all things masculine which manifested itself in that most supremely androcentric of institutions, the Christian faith. Instead, I took to paganism and a romantic notion of the Earth Goddess; the more I wanted to be a woman, the more my religious leanings reflected the eternal feminine. I say 'wanted to be a woman' because that's how it was, plain and simple. I didn't consider myself to have been born in the wrong body, I didn't accuse any divine being of making an almighty mess of things and, although I have more than a cursory knowledge of psychology, I'm not going looking for excuses there, either, and I'm certainly not going to claim that God intended me to be a woman. I hated being a man, as simple as that; I found it increasingly hard to relate to being a man and so, at the relatively tender age of 27, I decided to 'become' a woman – inasmuch as one can 'become' a woman. I did it because I was actually quite good at it, I did it because it made me feel a lot more comfortable with myself and I did it, believe it or not, for the reasons outlined above, as an act of rebellion. In a society whose values are, still, essentially masculine, I considered it vaguely subversive, a kick in the teeth for patriarchal values.

While I shall be eternally grateful to Simone de Beauvoir for her observation that 'women are made, not born' I would also accept that the relationship between behaviour and biology is a two-way process – the one informs the other and vice versa – and there are many aspects of 'womanhood' or 'femaleness' that I cannot experience. Some of these are biological – menstruation and motherhood, for example; others are historical – the experience of childhood and adolescence. I'm under no illusions as to the nature and extent of femaleness (my femininity is another matter altogether); I'm a socially and surgically constructed woman, but as far as I'm concerned that's better than not being a woman at all. If society treats me as a woman, then that's fine by me; I'm sure Ms de Beauvoir would agree.

And it's the socio-religious concepts of what make a woman that concern me and inform a theology that is clearly influenced – if not dominated – by my gender. Do faith and an understanding of the divine undergo changes as radical and far-reaching as that of the process of change occurring within both the body and the mind? The vast majority of transsexuals move from male to female but in doing so do they also reject the masculine values – within which I would nominally include Christianity – they were raised with?

I'm not so sure. In her scathing and not unwarranted attack on the 'sex-change industry' Janice Raymond argues that many male-to-female transsexuals constitute feminism's greatest enemy as, paradoxically, they frequently become hideously masculine caricatures of femaleness and represent a victory of the male construct of femininity over a genuinely liberating and empowering femininity (Raymond 1980). She has a point; in undergoing the transgendered process myself I accept that in the overall scheme of things I've done nothing to challenge the tyranny of gender – quite the opposite in fact. I've already admitted that gender exerts an undue influence over my theology and relationship with the divine. I might as well go the whole hog and confess that it exerts an undue influence over my entire life, no matter how successful I might be. I'm still a prisoner of gender, only the confining walls are now painted pink instead of blue.

Not only that. In acknowledging my persistent affection for the Catholic faith and my deep and long-lasting devotion to the Virgin Mary I'm aware that I'm also vulnerable to the accusation that in fleeing, in the most dramatic manner, from masculinity I am myself seeking solace in what many feminist theologians consider the ultimate male construct of repressive eternal feminine, Our Lady herself. You know what they say: hell hath no fury like the converted.

If only it were that simple. Why should the devil have all the best tunes?

Several years ago I was invited to an interview with *The Tablet* to contribute to its 'Church in the World' news service. I gave the editor an outline of my theology which, we broadly agreed, derived from a 'feminist-liberationist' perspective. Fair enough. *The Tablet* considers itself a forum for 'progressive, but responsible Catholic thinking' and I wasn't the first 'feminist-liberationist' to grace its pages. Imagine his surprise, then, when I remarked upon how much I loved the Latin Mass, that I believed in the Immaculate Conception of the Virgin Mary and the Virgin Birth and that I thought that some of the reforms of Vatican II and a continued emphasis on ecumenism were in danger of creating a kind of Catholicism *lite*, though I did also argue that the conception of Jesus was a lesbian event.

And that, of course, is not supposed to be the case. Here, on the one side, are the traditionalists and conservatives – the ultramontanists, Opus Dei and the like. Here, on the other, are the progressives and radicals – the feminist theologians and Catholic dissidents. Diametrically opposed: never the twain shall meet. I'm not sure which earns me greater disapproval: being a feminist theologian who's a Catholic with traditionalist leanings or being a Catholic with traditionalist leanings who's also a feminist theologian – or being a transsexual woman who claims to be a feminist theologian. Every which way I turn, there's always someone wanting to have a pop at me.

I was 29 when I started living as a woman 'full-time', as the transgendered vernacular would have it. One day I left the office as Simon and came back the next as Siân. It really was as simple as that; within 48 hours the fuss had died down and we all got on with our lives again.

Curiously enough, it was at that time that I began to flirt with Catholicism again; surreptitiously at first, not wishing to draw attention to myself and because I felt I didn't belong. Perhaps because I felt I'd transgressed some kind of 'natural law' and in doing so had forfeited any right to call myself a Catholic. I wasn't supposed to be there, I certainly wasn't supposed to receive the Holy Eucharist because people like me – sexual dissidents and gender renegades – have forfeited our right to belong. Like Eve, we have transgressed, surrendered to temptation and eaten the forbidden fruit. *Love the sinner, hate the sin*; the community reluctantly tolerates our presence as long as we remain safely ensconced on the periphery and don't kick up a fuss. In the Christian churches – with a few honourable exceptions – transsexuals are supposed to behave like Victorian children and be seen and not heard. Well, better not be seen at all, too. Sit at the back and don't expect to deliver the readings or lecture the Catholic Women's League on women and theology in Central America – though that's exactly what I did.

But it's all too easy to fall into the trap of condemning the Church, firing off letters and emails to the liberal media censuring its position on sex and sexuality and demanding that its participation in secular society should be drastically curtailed. I know I should be grateful that there exists, somewhere deep within the labyrinthine passages of the Passport Agency, a tiny little office whose sole purpose is to deal with requests from people like me. I am extremely grateful; my passport now declares me a female and if the passport says so, it must be true. Every other organization, public or private, seems to have a similar, tiny little office whose sole purpose is to make those equally tiny, little changes in documentation to reflect changes in gender. Christian orthodoxy can kick up a fuss until the cows come home but nobody appears to take much notice any more.

Several years ago, while working for a national mental health charity, I 'came out'. Not as a transsexual or pseudo-lesbian, no one batted an eyelid about that, but as a Catholic. There were those in that esteemed organization who'd have fired me on the spot, which just goes to show that secular socicty has its own version of *love the sinner, hate the sin.* Having gratefully accepted the state's complicity in my gender reassignment – it even paid for my surgery – I was accused, in effect, of biting the hand that fed me, of sleeping with the enemy.

Hallelujah. The state addresses me as Ms Siân Taylder so Ms Siân Taylder I must be. But the state – or rather society – doesn't hand out such plaudits without demanding something in return. Society, like the Church, has a curious relationship with what medical professionals like to call 'gender dysphoria' but the tabloid press prefers to call 'sex change' as in 'my sex-change hell' or, even more lasciviously, 'vicar in sex-swap bust-up'. Society grants me female status with the proviso that I keep quiet, know my place and never raise my head above the parapet again. That's the deal, but given the vaguely 'Carry-On' image of transsexuals in the Great British public's imagination, it's hardly likely that anyone's going to take me seriously. Women like me aren't supposed to appear in the full light of the public gaze unless, of course, as a subject of titillation and/or mild amusement.

All of which begs the question. What role, if any, do women like me have to play in the study of theology from a female or feminist perspective? There are those who would argue, with varying degrees of vehemence, none at all. That the mere reconstruction of a female body – and from a masculine perspective – does not qualify anyone to speak from a female point of view or on behalf of naturally born women who have suffered the slings and arrows of gender oppression since birth. 'Women' like me, they insist, should have their own space; *love the sinner, hate the sin.*

They have a point, but that clearly hasn't stopped me barging into the party anyway and making my voice heard. And while there are those who aren't entirely happy with my presence, there are plenty more who go along with Simone de Beauvoir. Whose is the authentic voice of the female experience in theology and religion? Who speaks for the dozens of Salvadoran women I've interviewed who live in rural and urban poverty and remain unrepresented socially, politically and theologically? Who speaks for the handful of lesbian and bisexual women among that group of poor women who, contrary to the assertions of left-wing leaders such as Daniel Ortega, do exist and are not an invention of the imperialist bourgeoisie? Who speaks for the four transgendered youths beaten to a pulp in El Salvador in December 2006 – an occurrence which is all too common in that and Central American republics? I can cope with parting shots from disapproving radical feminists and intransigent religious conservatives but when any theology purporting to foster social and sexual liberation turns the full force of its disapproval upon me, I might well look to the so-called enemy to give me covering fire.

In making the transition from a 'he' to a 'she' you quickly learn that the likes of Judith Butler were spot on in claiming that gender is nothing more than a social construct. You soon realize that life, *per se*, is nothing more than a socio-cultural charade and that you have to play along with the fraud and sustain levels of deceit that would get you convicted in a court of law. Gender is indeed a 'construct' and 'performance'. You have to adapt to the role but you also have to keep it up – on and off the stage – and that, believe me, is hard work.

It works on several levels; for example, when speaking Spanish I had to get used to referring to myself in the feminine, to say *soy inglesa* rather than *soy inglés*. But it can be more pernicious than that: there have been times when I've reinvented my own life story and played games with the past. Like Peter denying Christ, I've tried to convince people that Simon never existed, that I never knew him or that he'd somehow passed away. For heaven's sake, there have been times when I've managed to fool myself that Simon Taylder esquire and Ms Siân Lacey Taylder are entirely different creations.

But I suppose that, in a sense, they are.

I realize that in spending the best part of seven thousand words attempting to explain – and justify – my existence and the theology which underpins it I've come close to accusing just about everyone who feels a little uneasy with the concept of gender reassignment. Not only that, I've been rather belligerent – if not aggressive – in my own self-defence. Guilty as charged, m'lud. I've said it before and I'll say it again: attack is the best form of defence. Assert yourself, stand your ground and stake out your territory. Assume everyone is an adversary. Judge, first; only lower your guard when you know the coast is clear because for a woman like me everyone is a potential adversary.

And that's why, having been, in the course of my life, sniped at from each and every direction, I got my retaliation in first, even – especially – when it comes to theology and religion and while I've tried to reserve the full force of my anger for the usual suspects I can't help but fulminate against their radical counterparts who's attacks can be even more scathing and hurtful. I've no objection to theology getting personal but when a respected academic casually remarks that 'all transsexuals rape women's bodies by reducing the real female form to an artefact' (Raymond 1980, p. 308), then I feel compelled to defend myself with as much vigour as I can muster. It's a crude analogy that not only cheapens an argument that has some validity but gratuitously insults victims of rape. I don't mind being on the receiving end of criticism for being a transsexual – I'm not a victim; it was my decision and my decision alone to go through the process. What I do object to is bringing rape into the equation – as both a transsexual and a victim of rape I can tell you that any comparison is as odious as it is inappropriate.

Which brings us, nicely and symmetrically, back to the beginning; from Genesis to Revelation, from love the sinner to hate the sin. Give the sinner a pat on the head, offer her a cup of tea and whisper to her soothingly: 'There, there; you've learned you're lesson, you won't do that again, will you? Now run along, keep your pretty little head down and don't say another word.'

Only it doesn't matter if you do because nobody will take any notice of you, anyway. They'll shake their heads and say something along the lines of 'she's a freak, what does she know about political science/economics/ theology' (delete as applicable). It's not so long ago that women were being treated so patronizingly, still are, in fields as liberal as academia. Maybe I should just hold up my hands and say, 'now I know how it feels'.

Maybe not. Maybe I should forget about turning the other cheek and shout out: *ya basta*! – enough is enough.

Because I'm not making a plea for a specifically transsexual theology. Heaven knows, I've spent the last 12 years of my life trying to divest myself of labels rather than have any more pinned to me, and it's that pigeonholing that's the root of the problem. I have, of course, been taken with the utmost seriousness by academics of political science and theology as this chapter proves and, to a certain extent, I'm fulminating against an enemy that's as generic as it is invisible. But you see what 'they' are doing, don't you? *Love the sinner, hate the sin*? It's a not so subtle way of circumnavigating those of us they'd rather remain on the periphery because we – and I include transsexuals in this – are the sort of women your parents warned you about, the nightmare that wakes you, sweating, in the middle of the night.

You think I'm joking? How would you react if your son walked in and announced, out of the blue, that he wanted to become a woman? You're only human; you'd try to talk him out of it. Strange how liberal platitudes can suddenly dissolve into dust.

They would like to erase us from the face of the earth. They can't do it legally, they prefer not to resort to violence, but they'll do their damnedest to do it by stealth. They'll patronize you, ignore you, pretend you don't really exist. They'll convince society you're a non-person; you'll even begin to believe it yourself. You'll begin to resemble the title of Gabriel García Márquez's novel: 'nobody writes to the transsexual'. From there it's only a short step to paranoia and that, of course, is when they scent victory and move in for the kill.

Okay, maybe we, as transsexuals, deserve it but I'll tell you something for nothing. When they've finished with us they might well come looking for you!

References

Althaus-Reid, Marcella (2004), 'When God Is a Rich White Woman Who Does Not Walk: The Hermeneutical Circle of Mariology in Latin America', in *From Feminist Theology to Indecent Theology: Readings on Poverty, Sexual Identity and God* (London: SCM Press).

Campbell, Dennis (2006), 'B&B law sparks Bible backlash', *Observer* 26 March 2006, <http://www.guardian.co.uk/uk/2006/mar/26/gayrights.religion>.

Norton, John (2003), 'Vatican Says Sex Change Operation Does Not Change a Person's Gender', *Catholic News Service* 14 January 2003, <http://www.tgcrossroads.org/news/archive.asp?aid=599>.

Raymond, Janice (1980), *The Transsexual Empire: The Making of the She-Male*, London: The Women's Press.

Rosenberg, Mica (2008), 'Mexico transgender couple ties the knot, pushes law', <http://www.reuters.com/article/latestCrisis/idUSN17471304>.

Southam, Hazel (2001), 'Ban sex change ops, says church' *Independent* 14 January 2001, <http://www.independent.co.uk/news/uk/this-britain/ban-sex-change-ops-says-church-702085.html>.

Taylder, Siân Lacey (2008), *Death by Eyeliner: When Masculinity Goes Horribly Wrong*, <http://www.authonomy.com/ViewBook.aspx?bookid=854>.

6

God is a Many Gendered Thing: An Apophatic Journey to Pastoral Diversity

B. K. HIPSHER

> A good way to honour the Creator is to '*pay attention*' to what She has created.
>
> (Mollenkott 2008)

How do we pay attention to what God has created? How can we see the vast diversity of humanity and understand ourselves as 'created in the image of God' (Gen. 1. 26–8)? Can we embrace a liberative *imago Dei* that has the capacity to include the multiplicity of human reality . . . the range of skin colour, cultural identity and gender construction and performance? It is important to pay attention to what God has created so that we are careful to honour and respect the creation. For Christians who believe in an incarnational theology that includes the ongoing revelation of the Christic presence manifested in humanity. These questions are integral to moving from defining what God *is* and going on to some possibilities for defining what God *is not*.

Dionysius the Areopagite has historically been credited with the works that are also known as the writings of Pseudo-Dionysius. The author of these works invented the word 'hierarchy' to describe the practice of humans acting out power over one another in ecclesial structures (Pseudo Dionysius 1987, p. 1). The term has expanded to include any power structure embedded in business, social, academic and other secular organizations or systems. A hierarchy in any context sets one or more persons over and above other persons, usually in some kind of 'pecking order' that benefits those at the top with privilege. The consequence is that these privileges extend corollary oppressions to those at the lower end of the power scale. Dionysius rightly pointed to various religious and social structures of power over hierarchies as mirror images of those same cultural assumptions about who and what God or divinity itself is. Jews of the Hebrew Scriptures wrote about a monotheistic image of the one, omnipotent, God image. Greek and Roman ideas contained images of divine beings elevated to positions of power over the other less-divine people. These images of power over held together structures of power centred in small numbers of individuals making decisions for and about the rest of those 'under' their rule. And indeed the archetype of leader or king or patriarch holding power over others is as old as recorded human history.

It is only fitting then to take the other Dionysian position of negative theologies to begin to deconstruct the *imago Dei* of traditional or so-called orthodox Christianity. If we look at some traditional images of God perhaps we can begin to understand the connection between these images and our own ability and need to imagine a god who is relevant to our own lives. The Christian incarnational understanding of God's presence manifested in the person of Jesus of Nazareth has led us into some interesting assumptions about who and what God is.

God as Male

The male gender identification of Jesus and the attribution of his references to God as 'Father' served to codify a singular male image of God the Father. Perhaps more importantly God becomes 'big Daddy in the sky', making God in the image of human hierarchies of power over. Patriarchal images of God serve to reinforce ecclesial and social power structures that privilege men over women and assert that the image of male is more perfectly representative of God than the image of female. Expanding on this idea, Elizabeth Schüssler Fiorenza points out that, 'An understanding of patriarchy solely in terms of male supremacy and misogynist sexism is not able to articulate the interaction of racism, classism, and sexism in

Western militarist societies' (Fiorenza 1996, p. 163). It is inaccurate to attribute patriarchy to the responsibility of men only. Women do quite as much to hold together this system as men. And Dorothee Sölle unmasks the element of obedience to this patriarchal image of God supporting ecclesial and social structures that seek to control human bodies. 'The main virtue of an authoritarian religion is obedience and self-abrogation . . . in contrast with a humanitarian religion, where the chief virtue is self-realization and resistance to growth is the cardinal sin' (Sölle 1996, p. 53). When the objective of a religion is conformity to a uniform code of conduct and identity that is deemed 'normal' by the power structure, we are left with an image of God that reinforces any dominant cultural social power structure that privileges some over many. In Western societies the translation is simple: white, male, heterosexual, educated, middle- and upper-class people without physical, mental or emotional challenges are superior and must therefore rise to positions of power and privilege to 'take care of' the rest of us properly.

This dominant group has the power to make the rules for the rest of us. Any point of privilege within this structure allows the dynamic to persist. So that I, for instance, a white, female, lesbian, educated and middle class with few visual references to physical, mental or emotional challenges enjoy perceived privilege in the Church and society over a person of colour, who may be male but identifies as gay, exhibits effeminate or feminine characteristics, or who is less well educated, having more obvious physical, mental or emotional challenges. The web of privilege is cast. The power over dynamic that allows me to make the rules for you, without the benefit of your experience, is in operation. This liberation theology perspective is the first movement in the journey to diversity. We must first understand that God is not exclusively defined by the Western patriarchal image of white, male, heterosexual, educated, middle- and upper-class people without physical, mental or emotional challenges.

God as Female

Mary McClintock Fulkerson, in referring to the work of Rosemary Radford Ruether, sheds light on the problem of simply adding woman to the category of 'ideal humanity' (Fulkerson 1997, p. 108). Her discussion calls attention to the need for Feminist Theologies to carefully avoid the trap of affirming female images of God in a way that 'diminishes male humanity' (Fulkerson 1997, p. 109). She contends that simply shifting to female images of God or including female images of God reinforces a binary gender construct that supports normative heterosexuality and elevates it to the position of the divine nature of human beings.

> The feminist appeal to *imago Dei* becomes, then, affirmation that the world is divided into two kinds of people and what we want is respect for both kinds. But this implies that gender criticism is a kind of 'me too' theory. . .The continual affirming of man means that, minimally, what lurks behind the sign 'woman' in Ruether's formulation are certain constructions of heterosexual, male-desiring subjects who know their deep identities to be sexually female. (Fulkerson 1997, p. 109)

Here we face head on the spectre of heteronormativity even as we endeavour to blast open the idea that God can be only male. Virginia Ramey Mollenkott refers to the myriad ways binary gender constructs of male and female that imply a natural complimentarity have been used to visit injustices upon both men and women (Mollenkott 2001, p. 31). These images of complimentarity lock men and women into rigid gender performance roles that restrict men from displaying emotions and forbid women from entering the realms of politics, law, ecclesial authority, etc.

Tom Bohache explores postcolonial theory to illustrate further the damage dominant heteronormative ideals can visit on both men and women who do not identify as heterosexual.

> Postcolonial theory demonstrates that it is acceptable to question a received tradition. We are permitted to 'defy,' 'erode,' or 'supplant' the dominant readings of laws, scriptures, religious or political doc-

> trines, and texts of every kind, oral and written. In this sense, I believe it is crucial for gay and lesbian people to acknowledge that we have lived under a type of 'heterocolonialism' which has directed all of our thoughts, attitudes, beliefs, and customs toward compulsory heterosexuality from the moment of our birth, when we were assigned a gender by means of a blue or pink baby blanket. Whatever we did from then on was measured according to rigid gender roles, and deviation of a boy from his blue-blanket path or a girl from her pink-blanket path led to intimidation, punishment, and violence. (Bohache 2006)

God as Gay/Lesbian

If simply adding woman to the ideal human image of man produces the concept of complimentarity and reinforces a heteronormative binary construct then perhaps transgressing 'heterocolonialism' might release us from the dominant culture normative bind. Surely a concept of a Queer Christ gives us an incarnational image of diversity that opens up the possibilities that any one of us can relate to God in our spiritual search. Bob Goss explodes what he calls 'Christian homodevotion to Jesus' by calling attention to the practice of denying Jesus' sexuality as a way of negating eroticism in all of us and discounting our sexuality. This allows the Church to control how, with whom and in what context we are allowed to have sexual relations. In this scenario celibacy is elevated to the preferred state of humanity, discounting the gift and beauty of human sexual expression, except for the purpose of procreation (Goss 2002, pp. 113–15). Goss gives us images of male-male and female-female love that allow homosexual-identifying people to find themselves in the images of a Queer Christ who opens up the heteronormative image of complimentarity and allows for the expression of love that does not conform.

Further, Goss moves on to expose the inadequacies of gay/lesbian theological perspectives pointing out the exclusion of bisexual and transgender identities.

> While gay/lesbian theological works have concentrated mainly on questions of homosexuality, queer theory has expanded the realm of

investigation to sexual desire, paying close attention to cultural construction of categories of normative and deviant sexual behaviors. Queer theory expanded the scope of its queries to all kinds of behaviors linked to sexuality, including gender-bending and nonconventional sexualities. (Goss 2002, pp. 223–4)

God as Transgender

It is not enough to include homosexual identity and sexual expression in an expanded *imago Dei*. We must be critical enough to open up the possibilities for human expression to include the full range and fluidity of human sexuality and sexual expression and embrace the concept of surgical and hormonal gender reassignment.

While the category bisexual may be adequately self-explanatory it may be helpful to expand on the term transgender. Virginia Ramey Mollenkott explores various expressions of transgender identity in her book *Omnigender* (2001). She illuminates the variety of transgender expression that can fall into such a category. Transvestites, drag queens and drag kings who dress as the alternate gender to their biology, and intersexual people of all biological and hormonal/chemical/chromosomal varieties are included in the term transgender. And of course transsexual people who have undergone surgical or hormonal gender reassignment procedures also are included in the term (Mollenkott 2001, pp. 38–77). It goes without saying that any attempt to categorize sexual expression within such a diverse group simply makes our heteronormative binary constructed heads spin. And questions of what sexuality has to do with spirituality are bound to arise in our heterocolonialized minds.

I have endeavoured to articulate the list of images that we can discard as what God is not. This list includes male, female, male and female complimentarity, and gay/lesbian images that continue to hold together a binary gender construct that excludes transgender identity. Yet how do those among us who understand ourselves as predominantly one or the other gender and who fall relatively neatly into hetero- or homosexual expressions of human intimacy deal with the image of a transgender God whose identity and embodied expression is free to move fluidly from one to the other to the other? And why is the issue of sexuality even an issue in theological discussions? Isn't theology concerned with the spiritual connection of God and humanity and our spiritual relationship to each other?

I am prepared to assert that the very fact that Christianity is based in an incarnational theology that assigns divinity to the person of Jesus of Nazareth demands that we deal with the human embodiment of diversity in sexual biological presentation and our embodiment as sexual beings. For progressive Christians like myself, orthodox understandings of a singular incarnation of the Christ as Jesus *only* notwithstanding, every human being is an expression of the Christic spirit or presence of God. It is our duty and privilege as pastors and sojourners on a spiritual path to understand and support each other in our vast multiplicity of embodiment. To do otherwise discounts the particularity of our individuality and runs the risk of reinforcing those pesky patriarchal/hierarchical ideas that set one group over the other and allow those in power to make the rules by which everyone must live.

A *Trans*-God

We see this kind of drama playing out in various Christian denominations by excluding gay, lesbian, bisexual and transgender people from membership in the worst cases. These people are simply pushed out of their faith communities when they come 'out' as something other than binary gender-construct, heterosexual-identified persons. In some cases homosexual couples are tolerated if they conform to the binary construct in other ways of dress, action, etc. For instance if a gay male couple dresses appropriately as men, perform male-gender construction and form a nuclear family unit complete with marriage bonds and promises of monogamy they may attain a level of acceptance having tapped into so many intersections of the dominant cultural heteronormative identity. Another acceptable manifestation might be a lesbian couple where neither of the women dress too masculinely or too femininely, perhaps they adopt or give birth to one or more children and, again, marry and perform the heteronormative couple signifiers such as monogamy. Where the rubber meets the road is when a gay man transitions to a female gender identity, with or without surgery, and doesn't 'pass' well . . . for example, when a male-to-female (M-to-F) transsexual continues to have a deep voice, masculine movements or attitudes, yet identifies and dresses as a woman. Or when one partner in a nice lesbian couple begins to take testosterone, has chest reconstruction surgery to remove breasts and proceeds to dress, act and live as a man. At this point most Christian denominations freeze. If they tolerate the person at all, there is no community outreach, no sense of inclusion, no image of God in the context of the church community with which this particular incarnation of the Christic presence can identify. More overt rejection of a person like this can include emotional, spiritual and physical violence visited on the transsexual person in the name of keeping the ranks of the faithful 'clean' and 'holy'.

It is precisely because a transgender image of God is so unsettling to most people that we are compelled to argue for it. If God cannot be male only, female only, male and female complementary composite then what is the apophatic conclusion? I believe that we are compelled to image God in the ever-changing, shifting, diverse and multiple transgender realities that human beings embody. To encapsulate God into any single gender identity or sexual expression limits the possibilities of God's manifestations in humanity. Furthermore a human embodiment that is outside these limited images of God would be open to attack and violence in the name of forcing conformity to the 'natural' ways of God. But is an image of a transgender God still too limiting, too small, to hold the God of the universe? The simple answer is yes.

We need a *trans*-God alright . . . one that *trans*gresses all our ideas about who and what God is and can be, one that *trans*ports us to new possibilities for how God can incarnate in the multiplicity of human embodiments, one that *trans*figures our mental images from limitations, one that *trans*forms our ideas about our fellow humans and ourselves, one that *trans*cends all we know or think we know about God and about humanity as the *imago Dei*.

How do we get there?

As we have seen it is important to break down the traditional, so-called orthodox, images of God as male only. This is the first movement toward the *trans*-God. When we tear down images of God restricted to male gender identity and desexualized to elevate celibacy above sexual expression of human love we open the possibility that people who do not conform to this image are worthy of love and respect. Women become real people in and outside the Church. Their leadership is respected and valued. Their voices are heard. Their names are remembered. Moreover, tearing down the heteronormative male-female complimentarity model opens the way for gay, lesbian and bisexual people to enjoy the same kinds of acceptance and respect. This move is not only good for the institution or dominant culture system itself but is a great source of self-respect allowing for the healing of internalized misogyny and homophobia that pervades many of our friends and family in society and Church.

The second move is the acceptance of the possibility of a transgender image of God. This *trans*-God image has the capacity to move fluidly between gender identities and sexualities. This image of God allows every incarnation of the Christic presence in humanity to be valued and respected. An image of God that allows for this kind of diversity would never allow, much less promote, violence of any kind toward any person. A *trans*-God image would compel each of us to stretch and search for an understanding of anyone we consider 'other'. This paradigm shift would open up our minds to the joy of considering the limitless possibilities for human diversity rather than holding our minds hostage to limited images of the *imago Dei* and the accompanying angst that we carry when faced with the mulitiplicity of human embodiment set against a limited image of God.

The third move involves our ability to look inside ourselves and accept who we are and how we're made and what our preferences and tendencies are with relation to gender and sexuality without carrying the enormous weight of what we think we're 'supposed' to be as Christians. This self-inflicted, self-denying, self-hatred is the worst kind of selfish and self-centred activity that disconnects us first from each other and potentially interferes with our relationship with God. Our own spiritual connection to God is part of the link that is necessary to spiritual growth, maturity and health. Acceptance and celebration of our own diversity allows us to grow and change, moving between gender identities and sexualities if we feel compelled, taking away the limitations that we place on each other to 'choose up sides' and be true to our identity in politics, society and the Church. We move into a realm where I can self-identify as a lesbian today, as a heterosexual if I fall in love with a man, as a transgender person if I experience myself transitioning from a female identity without any fear of whether I will be homosexual or heterosexual when I transition from one gender to the other. Perhaps we will one day arrive at a place where the antiquated ideas of binary gender constructs begin to be less important than the character of the person and their ability to show and receive love.

Real life

These lessons were difficult for me, and my journey along this path has been long in some respects and short in others. My first encounter with a transgender person was in the mid-1970s when I was in undergraduate school and just coming out to myself and others as a lesbian. I worked for a man who was an F-to-M transsexual and who did not hide this fact from me. He did not seem in any way unusual to me but looking back I certainly did not personally identify with him as a peer. He was something 'other' than what I was. He was a woman who had become a man. I was a woman struggling in the feminist movement of those days without an understanding of the larger context.

Many years later, and not so many years ago, I was attending a retreat at Kirkridge Retreat Center in Pennsylvania. This retreat is specifically designed for gay, lesbian, bisexual and transgender (GLBT) people. A few years ago, I arrived and met a woman who looked like a lesbian, talked like a lesbian, even dressed like a lesbian (whatever that means) but identified herself as a heterosexual ally to GLBT people. At the same retreat an M-to-F transsexual was also in attendance. Except for my brief associations with drag queens in my youth, I had never (knowingly) encountered an M-to-F transsexual, certainly not one who was willing to declare it openly and one who did not 'pass' particularly well. This woman appeared to be a very butch woman wearing very feminine clothes, an image that was wholly unfamiliar to me within my realm of experience and thought. Later in the weekend when time came to choose participants for the final evening 'fish bowl' or panel presentation great care was taken to assure gender parity in the choices. As the featured participants gathered, three males and three females filed in to participate in the final evening's presentation. As I looked at the females there was only one lesbian, the heterosexual ally and the M-to-F transsexual on the female side. I shook my head and commented to my female partner that this was 'typical' . . . one lesbian and three gay men. In my essentialist mindset I completely discounted any identification with the other two women and certainly didn't think I had anything in common with the gay men in the group.

As the participants began to speak, I heard the experience of some of the gay men, and their fears and hopes and dreams began to sound very familiar to me. Their yearning to know God's presence in their lives was the same as mine. Their overwhelming compulsion to try to conform to as many of society and Church norms as they possibly could was similar to my own. And their tendency to discount their own experience because an image of God as a gay man was hard to find was a mirror of my struggle to find myself in a church that had no images of women, particularly lesbian women. A Jesus devoid of sexuality was a difficult image for me and for these gay men with whom to identify.

The heterosexual-identified female ally spoke of her own struggle to maintain her identity within the GLBT community as a heterosexual. She described the suspicion with which lesbians who think she's hiding behind the privilege of heterosexual identification often regard her. And she described in detail the devastating price she pays in the heterosexual world for daring to stand up for GLBT people's rights in and out of the Church.

Then came the most stunning revelation of the evening. The M-to-F transsexual calmly related the disrespect with which she is often treated in all sorts of social and church contexts. She warmly smiled at her roommate for the weekend, the heterosexual ally, as she told us all that this particular weekend was the first time in her life she had ever been included with the women . . . the first time she had been afforded the privilege of sharing a room with another woman, staying in a woman's residence hall, sharing shower and washroom facilities with women. This was the first time she had ever been shown the courtesy of respecting the gender identity she understood herself to be. Needless to say, my life and attitudes were changed that night and have remained so. Changed not because I encountered some magnificent human beings who opened my eyes to human diversity. Changed by the Christic presence of these particular peculiar incarnations that opened my spirit to a vision of the *imago Dei* that I had never imagined. And my life continues to be changed, by Abigail, Kate, Eta, Chris, Cameron, Jacob, Michael and others. My image of God was changed and in the process my expectations of humanity were changed. I began to get a glimpse of what it means to allow the Christic presence to inhabit my spirit. I began to get a glimpse of the commonwealth of God coming alive in the midst of my human family. When I pay attention to what God has created my image of God transcends the limits of the dominant culture and allows me to experience the incarnation of particular peculiarities that enrich my spiritual life.

References

Bohache, Thomas (2006), 'Empire Meets Eros: A Queer (De)Construction', unpublished paper (American Academy of Religion, 'Theology & Religious Reflection' Section).

Fiorenza, Elizabeth Schüssler (1996), 'Breaking the Silence – Becoming Visible', in Elizabeth Schüssler Fiorenza, ed., *The Power of Naming: A Concilium Reader in Feminist Liberation Theology* (London: SCM Press), pp. 161–74.

Fulkerson, Mary McClintock (1997), 'Contesting the Gendered Subject', in Rebecca S. Chopp and Sheila Greeve Davaney, eds, *Horizons in Feminist Theology: Identity, Tradition, and Norms* (Minneapolis: Fortress Press), pp. 106–23.

Goss, Robert E. (2002), *Queering Christ: Beyond Jesus Acted Up* (Cleveland, OH: The Pilgrim Press).

Mollenkott, Virginia Ramey (2001), *Omnigender: A Trans-religious Approach* (Cleveland, OH: The Pilgrim Press).

Mollenkott, Virginia Ramey (2008), 'Gateways and Growth Spurts', unpublished lecture at the annual 'Christian People of the Rainbow' retreat for GLBT people, their families and allies at Kirkridge Retreat Center in June 2008.

Pseudo-Dionysius (1987), *Complete Works,* trans. Colm Luibheid (Mahwah: Paulist Press).

Sölle, Dorothee (1996), 'Paternalistic Religion', in Elizabeth Schüssler Fiorenza, ed., *The Power of Naming: A Concilium Reader in Feminist Liberation Theology* (London: SCM Press), pp. 150–60.

7

The Butch Woman inside James Dean, or 'What kind of a *person* do you think a girl wants?'

MARIE CARTIER

James Dean made only three films in his short life, and yet he remains one of our most famous and durable stars. Why? It is my thesis that James Dean's masculinity was a filmic translation of a masculinity he saw created by butch women of the 1950s, and that was he very interested in portraying and helping to create the beginnings of what we now call 'queer nation'.

'He was the first rebel,' Sal Mineo, co-star of *Rebel*, said. 'He was the first guy to ask, Why?' (Martinetti 1995, p. 123)

Through his 'transgendered' performance Dean was implicitly asking 'why?' Why was gender set up the way it was? He presented the first glimpse to the general public of this new type of masculinity that was being created and lived by butch women in urban culture. He was the messenger of that masculinity to the culture at large. This message proved so attractive to heterosexual culture that it formed the basis for what we call the 'New Man' who appeared out of the 1950s – the man who could cry and have feelings.

This study analyses how Dean's portrayal deconstructs his own life, and how with the strict Production Code of the 1950s the cast and crew of the 1955 *Rebel without a Cause* pulled off the unique feat of filming so many coded, but still very 'queer', signs or indications.

In a two-gender system in which any gender trait deviation is suspect, a 'queer nation' is almost unimaginable, therefore very hard to discuss without sliding back into talking about 'the individual', who is having trouble.

Stewart Stern, the writer of *Rebel*, said that, while the movie was called *Rebel without a Cause*, it was not the rebels who were without a cause. The misfit youths had a very definite and articulated cause, to find 'a place', even if, as Dean stated in the movie, 'just for one day'.

The rebels did have a cause, and were only perceived as not having one. That is why Dean was and is so admired by butch women, and why I argue Dean himself admired butch women.

Jenni Olsen, a butch woman, wrote: 'On screen, tomboys were socially acceptable. As a young butch dyke coming out in 1986, I couldn't find anything . . . I turned to Marlon Brando and James Dean as my role models of butchness' (Olsen 1994, p. 58).

Why is it important to attribute Dean's portrayal to a slyly constructed butch? Because it has been historically levelled against butch women that they are and have been 'acting like men' – when in fact, I believe, the opposite. The New Man, since the Second World War, acts like a woman – a butch woman.

In a longer study on this topic (Cartier 1999), I examine why lesbians distanced themselves from the 'butch' image in the 1970s, why they tentatively claim it today, and conclude with an analysis of the butch persona occasionally presented on screen. In the 1950s, when we saw her at all she had to be lawless and immoral, as in the 1958 *A Touch of Evil* with Mercedes McCambridge's uncredited role as a Mexican butch, who says, 'Lem-me stay. I wanna watch', when the gang of boys she runs with are raping a girl. Or she could be a squeaky clean, living with a woman 'butch soldier' as long as she was straight by the end, as in Doris Day's *Calamity Jane*.

Nicholas Ray, *Rebel*'s director, prior to directing *Rebel*, also directed *Johnny Guitar*, infamous for its portrayals of masculine, that is, 'butch' cowgirl women, McCambridge opposite Joan Crawford.

Many questions can be asked of this particular canon of 1950s films. For instance, if *Johnny Guitar* is unique in the role reversal of female-to-male roles, why have we never speculated that the same director who did both *Johnny* and *Rebel* may be uniquely interested in gender-role reversal, especially as it concerns the portrayal of 'butch' and 'masculinity'? If today some believe that gender-role playing means parody to learn something, not necessarily parody to mock, then we can ask, what can be learned about the male role from watching Crawford in *Johnny Guitar*, and what can be learned about the female role from watching Dean in *Rebel*?

The longer study analyses these comparative implications, as well as a possible systematic theology that Dean created in his very original approach to method acting – a self-identified moment-to-moment system of acting, and of living.

In this paper, however, I am most interested in asking why did this performance and this star speak to, as noted below, 'an entire generation'?

Rebel without a Cause, written by Stewart Stern and directed by Nicholas Ray, starred Natalie Wood, Sal Mineo and James Dean, in what Leonard Maltin and other critics agree was probably Dean's 'seminal performance'. Maltin summarizes it as a 'portrait of youthful alienation [which] spoke to an entire generation'.

How and why did *Rebel* speak to an entire generation, and what was it saying to them? What was it about a rebel and perhaps a rebellion that was so attractive? *Rebel* is the focus here because I believe it illustrates Dean's masculinity as modelled on that of butch women, and a new queer consciousness that was born and presented to the public through the gaze of this film.

If the film *Rebel* spoke to an entire generation, what did it speak about? It has been noted often that *Rebel* was the first film to identify 'teen-hood' as a valid life phase. Perhaps, however, what Dean was suggesting was that the transition from child to adult, or teen, not only existed but that it was particularly challenging because the rigidity of gender roles were especially acute at the time this film was made.

Dean himself challenged these gender roles, on and off screen. According to *Out of All Time: A Gay and Lesbian History*, Hedda Hopper once asked Dean how he avoided the draft, and Dean responded, 'I kissed the medic.' Dean avoided the draft by admitting he was gay . . .

It is my assumption that Dean was in fact a 'rebel', a bisexual who lived, however, almost exclusively as a homosexual. All the evidence suggests this to be true, including the three biographies of Dean that are the most authoritative and comprehensive.[1]

Dean created a 'new man', on screen, one he did not necessarily embody in his own life. As an actor schooled in 'the method' where did he see that persona to portray it so powerfully on screen? Was it his own invention? As a method actor Dean would have to see this persona modelled in order to 'invent' a persona for himself to bring forth in his craft. Where was he exposed to this 'new man'?

Consider this excerpt from *Culture Clash: The Making of Gay Sensibility*:

> The 1950s were the decade of the 'organizational man.' By organizing and defining themselves, homosexuals reassured straight people terrified by the Kinsey Report: they were visible . . . the majority of homosexuals who formed this visible subculture were effeminate men, butch women, obvious queens and the drags who gained a positive identity, but who were also the targets of disdain from mainstream culture. (Bronski 1984, pp. 79–80)

The need for these images to be constructed so that identification with them would not be obvious identification with homosexual elements is apparent when one remembers that in the 1950s one could be sent to jail if one did not have on three gender-appropriate articles of clothing. Being

1 From my research these would be the following: the most recent and authoritative is Alexander, 1997; second, by one of Dean's young male lovers, Gilmore 1997; and third, Martinetti 1995.

Gilmore dedicates the book to his wife, Marie, but is also very open about his relationship with Dean. He sees himself as bisexual, and chronicles affairs he and Dean had with women, with each other, and affairs that Dean had with other men.

Martinetti's book clearly is meant to document the relationship that was the most seminal for Dean's career, that with the older film-maker, Rogers Brackett, who requested that details of their relationship be kept secret until after his death. From all accounts, Dean dropped this man from his life once he 'made it'. Martinetti was granted the only interview that Brackett gave before his death.

transgressive in gender was against the law. That these gender outlaws risked being sent to jail, were often sent to jail and often continued their behaviour after returning from jail announced a powerful subculture in urban mid-century America. The visible gay culture was publicly disdained by the mainstream. However, that attractive elements from this subculture – such as a new masculinity – might be mainstreamed into the culture at large through a messenger like James Dean, who was believed to be a straight male, would not have been deemed possible. I am suggesting that it was possible and that Dean's portrayal is one way that the new masculinity created by butch women did in fact enter the mainstream.

Recent information has allowed us to substantiate some of the gay elements of *Rebel* – notably the published admissions by Dean and Mineo that they were both gay and/or bisexual. However, I am concerned here with the elements that we do not 'see'. What homosexual elements are people usually responding to in *Rebel*?

Stewart Stern, *Rebel*'s screenwriter, said:

> If I were doing it today [writing *Rebel*] I would want to make Plato think he was gay, and deal with that relationship. Jim Stark was not that way. But one of the reasons Plato was an outsider in that school was because people called him fag.

As many other gay analyses of the film have said, according to *Out of All Time*, 'The homosexual subtext is clear through the film – even though at the film's end, Dean gets Natalie Wood and Sal Mineo (Plato) gets shot' (Hopper 1984, p. 105).

My question is, *what* homosexual subtext is 'clear' throughout this film? Until this time, vulnerability embodied within a biologically gendered man, or embodying the 'new masculinity', as James Dean as Jim Stark does in *Rebel*, had not been seen on film.

Culture Clash suggests that:

> The war . . . changed the way Hollywood portrayed men. The three actors who most clearly represented this changed image were Marlon Brando, Montgomery Clift, and James Dean. It is no accident that

> both Dean and Clift were primarily homosexual and that Brando was a self-proclaimed bisexual. What all three brought to the screen was . . . the promise of an eroticism that was pliant and engaging: the strong, silent, rugged American male would never be the same. (Bronski 1984, p. 104)

Why was the portrayal of men changed after the Second World War? What happened at home, during the war, that changed the way that men were portrayed? How did the portrayal of masculinity change?

During the war, there were legions of women who for the first time were legitimately employed in plants and factories and, since they had gained economic freedom, they also gained the freedom to create a new type of 'masculinity' – embodied within a female biology – the 'butch' identity.

For the most part, butches dated femmes, a new type of woman, a woman who was proud of having sexual desire and able to construct a life in the repressed 1950s where that desire could be expressed and fulfilled. This construct was known as butch–femme.

In urban areas this type of coupling was visible to the mainstream culture, but it had never been previously presented on screen. This type of gender arrangement was not accessible to heterosexual men to emulate, unless they had access to gay culture. Straight men could, however, begin to emulate this new masculinity – part of which was honouring and encouraging a woman's desire – by virtue of Dean's performance providing the example.

Dean, Clift and Brando, as members of the gay community, had access to that community – particularly Dean, who was admittedly gay, did not go to the war, frequented gay clubs and delivered it via the cinema to the general population. This portrayal I believe changed the face of masculinity.

Where did Dean find the material for this important portrayal?

In 1955, homosexuality was illegal. Homosexuality was not removed from the American Psychological Association's list of mental diseases until 1973. In 1955 butch lesbians and their femme girlfriends would have made up a large percentage of any criminally institutionalized youth (or adult) population. This condition was definitely validated in the best of the women's prison-genre movies of the period, for example, the 1950 award-winning, *Caged*. Whether or not the lesbian portrayal is accurate in these movies is another question, but that lesbians populated criminal institutions was fairly well established. A large constituency of lesbian inmates were cross-dressing butches who 'crossed' the existing laws against homosexuality and then found themselves incarcerated and/or behind bars.

Ray and Stern, director and writer of *Rebel,* did have access to portrayals of butch women. Ray stated that he visited Juvenile Hall and interviewed social workers, psychiatrists, and juvenile offenders. He did this to find out what teenagers in places like that wanted. If they had a voice, what would they say? More than anything, Ray said, the movie was about the desire for the world to understand them. Said Ray, 'This movie is about a kid who wants to have one day that is not confused' (Martinetti 1995, pp. 120–1).

Part of what the confusion was for Dean I argue is that he saw a masculinity in butch women that was outlawed in heterosexual men, and was not strongly portrayed in gay men. As gay women were more transgressive by being masculine, so too were gay men more transgressive by being feminine. The femme lesbian and the butch gay man were still iconoclasts. Dean, however, had access to butch women – as friends, possibly 'protectors', of his space and others' space within the bar culture and, since he and the other men named above were actors, they had the freedom to act like butches – a freedom straight men lacked without the implicit permission provided by their performances.

Dean had a history of attaching himself to strong women, possibly butch women. Although it is hard to verify their sexuality, we can verify his history with women who embodied examples of what we would tend to call, especially in that period, masculine characteristics.

One example of his bond to female friends, and his allegiance to such friends, is illustrated when as a youth in the 1940s Dean refused to play basket ball on his home team in Indiana if his friend Melba was not allowed to play (Alexander 1997, p. 38).

As a young adult, Dean met Chris White, a woman with whom he shared an audition scene for admission to the prestigious Actor's Studio in his agent Jane Deacy's office. He noticed a young woman, wearing a red baseball cap, typing. Not many people wore a red baseball cap in an office in New York City. When he asked who she was, she snapped at him, 'Can't you see I'm busy?' This exchange commenced their fast friendship. According to reports, Jimmy wanted to walk out on the audition once the day arrived, but Chris said, 'Listen you little wretch, you're not going to louse up my audition. We're here now, and we're going through with it. *Now get out there.*' (Alexander 1997, pp. 107–9). They made the cut, and the rest is history.

Jimmy had many women like this in his life, women who transcended the gender codes of the period, by being more assertive, initiating and bold than was normally associated with the feminine gender. Among these bold women in Dean's life was Eartha Kitt, the person in real life who called him 'Jamie'. Interestingly this is the name that the gay character Plato, 'invents' for Jim in *Rebel* with the stipulation that only the people Jim really likes are allowed to call him Jamie (Stern 1955, pp. 33 and 56–62).[2] (This was changed from the original script which read, 'only . . . his mother calls him Jamie'.)

Lili Kardell, one of Dean's favourite 'dates' and one who liked to 'ride like hell' with Dean on his motorcycle, once gave him a gift of a new oil filter for his Porsche (Gilmore 1997, p. 134).

One of Jimmy's movie-star 'girlfriends', Ursula Andress, was compared to Brando in terms of her transgressive nature. Andress appeared in a photo with Dean actually giving the finger to the press, a very unladylike gesture. Reportedly, they often appeared in public, dressed in similar outfits, Ursula apparently clad in some form of masculine attire (Alexander 1997, p. 203, photo 204).

2 Note: many of the quotes from the movie cited in this study were not written by the listed writer, Stewart Stern (as is usual for most films). A line-by-line comparison made of the filmed version and the published screenplay indicates that the most rewrites occurred in the Judy/Judy's father story, the Jim's father/Jim storyline, Plato/Jim friendship story and *the love scenes between Judy and Jim.*

According to others, including Stern himself, Nicholas Ray, the director, allowed the actors, in the tradition of the Actor's Theatre, where Dean was trained, to improvise. *Since there was no other writer on the set, it is most likely that much of the rewritten material was the invention of the actors themselves, with the aid of Ray.*

Jimmy explained his sexual dynamic to Jonathan Gilmore, one of his male lovers, saying, 'I'm not active . . . I'm passive.' Later Gilmore wrote, 'we shared a look, a look that said, "If one of us were a girl, we would have been able to have a romance"' (Alexander 1997, pp. 131–7).

The concept of a butch-type gay male was not common in the 1950s. Dean would tangle later on the set of *Giant* with Rock Hudson, a more 'traditional' gay male. At this time the traditional gay male often appeared in drag at his parties, very unlike the traditional heterosexual male Hudson portrayed on screen.

As stated earlier, I believe that Dean, acting in *Rebel*, was acting as a butch woman. I believe that this persona, cloaked in the guise of his fictional heterosexuality, gave heterosexual men the permission to learn the 'new masculinity' that had been created during the war by butch women.

Of course, this learning curve could never be deconstructed in its time. Today the readings of the film that attribute the only homo-eroticism to the non-sexual protective alliance between Plato and Jim, Sal Mineo and James Dean, totally ignore the strong butch–femme portrayal that Jim and Judy, James Dean and Natalie Wood, provide.

Consider the scene in the opening of *Rebel* when Jim, upon entering the high school, mistakenly enters the women's room and then backs up and uses the men's room, checking the sign on the door first. What are we to make of that scene? Knowing that early scenes like that in films are meant to set up exposition regarding how we are to view this character's history, how should we interpret this action? This action is intercut with this, quoted from *Masked Men: Masculinity and Men in the Movies of the Fifties*:

> . . . shots of Plato opening his locker to comb his hair, catching sight of Jim in a mirror fastened to the inside of the door . . . Jim's image in the mirror . . . displaces a pin-up photo of Alan Ladd, which initially can be seen in Plato's locker. Plato's desiring look at Jim, establishes the homo-erotic ground of the friendship that will begin in the next scene at the planetarium . . . [and] sexualizes the boy's masculinity crisis. (Cohan 1997, pp. 253–4)

However, what is the homo-erotic ground here? What if we read Jim as butch? Is Jim in a masculinity crisis, or are we as the audience 'in crisis'– attempting to reconcile his unique identity/identification with established gender delineations? Why are we reading his confusion in the constrained gender world portrayed, as *his* problem? When in reality Jim's confusion is not his problem, it is our problem. The personality of Jim Stark reads as well rounded, not hot tempered, and trying to make sense of a nonsensical world. I believe Dean created in his character's persona the life he was actually struggling to lead – a person who accepts himself, but longs for a sense of belonging and acceptance in a world where he need not check the restroom signs.

Again from *Masked Men*:

> Plato's eroticizing viewpoint of Jim, comparable to Judy's enables the film to dramatize the bisexuality underlying this rebel boy's difference . . . Plato's death . . . the final link that leads to Jim's romance with Judy . . . disavows early implication of sexual rebellion; as far as the narrative closure is concerned, the desire of one boy for another literally amounts to a dead end. (Cohan 1997, pp. 253–4)

This is where I believe much of the theory falls short regarding this film. Because we cannot read Jim as queer, we cannot see what Dean is doing with Judy – enacting with the actor Natalie Wood the relationship he saw butch women enact with femmes in the urban subculture of the period, namely, in the bars of New York and the streets of Greenwich Village, West Hollywood, etc. His relationship with Judy *is* 'queer', in that time period, and their romance begins as soon as they meet, not after Plato's death. It is queer, different, in fact it is the most different relationship Judy has ever had with a boy – if Dean is playing 'a boy', for I believe, Dean is playing a butch.

I believe this is why in the reviews of *Boys Don't Cry*, the 1998 film about the real-life 1993 murder of Brandon Teena, a cross-dressing butch who was passing as a man, the following comparisons were made.

From *Variety*:

> The poignant and candid *Boys Don't Cry* can be seen as a *Rebel without a Cause* for these culturally diverse and complex times, with the two misfit girls enacting a version of the James Dean–Natalie Wood romance with utmost conviction, searching like their 50's counterparts, for love, self-worth, and a place to call home. (Levy 1999)

From the *Boston Phoenix*:

> A tremendous performance by Hilary Swank depicts Brandon as Thelma, Louise and James Dean rolled into one. (Heller 1999, p. 51)

I don't think in the world of this film specifically that Jim desires Plato, so much as Jim desires a queer *world* in which people like Plato can be safe. He desires a world where 'deviants' like Plato, Thelma and Louise and Brandon Teena can be safe, and where he can have a relationship with a girl like Judy that is not based on 'chickie runs' and masculine performance. For instance, Jim desires Judy, and wants to liberate her from an incestuous home. This is commonly a butch fantasy/sometimes reality. This theme is not common in heterosexual literature – the young man rescuing the daughter from an abusive, even incestuous father but it is a common theme in lesbian literature, particularly in stories featuring a butch. For example, Chea Villanueva's 'The Bad Girl', from *Bulletproof Butches*, is a short story that describes a woman going to prison because she kills the father who molests her girlfriend (Villanueva 1997). A strong lesbian saving another woman from male abuse, and in the process that woman discovering her own lesbianism is (when we have seen lesbians at all in recent movies) a common theme. Among these portrayals are the aforementioned Brandon Teena saving Lana in *Boys Don't Cry*, Shug saving Celie in *The Color Purple* and Idgie saving Ruth in *Fried Green Tomatoes*.

In *Rebel*, this rescue 'fantasy' is played out not only in saving Judy from her father but also in wanting to protect the mansion – the 'safe' place – from a gang of straight, homophobic boys who are intent on roughing up Plato and Jim.

Where does the construct of family fall when you are transgressive? Can one create a personal idea of family within a binary system that regulates this relational concept? On 24 February 1996, regular Norm McDonald appeared on *Saturday Night Live* in front of a blowup of *USA Today*'s cover story of the death of Brandon Teena and said, 'In Nebraska a man was sentenced for killing a female crossdresser who had accused him of rape and two of her friends. Excuse me if this sounds harsh, but in my mind, they all deserved to die' (<http://www.glaad.org>).

Even though this show is a satire, his comments mirrored a large percentage of the US population at the time – especially those of Midwest America, where the murder took place, and many say was allowed to take place. The police of Lincoln, Nebraska, did not arrest Brandon Teena's accused rapists after Teena reported the rape; they were finally arrested only after they murdered Teena, apparently not such an 'easy' charge to sit idle on as rape. In the light of this type of prejudice, is it any wonder that Dean, in 1955, wanted to create an alternative 'family' – as many queer people have been literally forced to do? I think the ability to create a new family is much more difficult than to love someone of the same sex, as difficult as that is, and more threatening – as evidenced by the recent American nation-wide debates over gay marriage.

When we de-eroticize the Jim/Judy relationship, in favour of seeing eroticism solely in the relationship with Plato, are we denying in this film the world of butch–femme, or are we ignorant of it? We read solely male homosexuality because it is the only thing we know to read, because we impose the assumed known outside sexualities of the actors, Dean and Mineo, upon the characters they are portraying. But in the world of the film, what is being tried is the creation of a kind of 'queer nation', which includes a butch–femme portrayal.

Consider the following filmed screenplay excerpt from *Rebel without a Cause*:

> Judy asks Jim . . . 'is this what it's like to love somebody?'
>
> Jim, 'I don't know.'
>
> Judy, 'What kind of a *person* do you think a girl wants?'
>
> Jim, 'A *man*?'

Judy, '*Yes* . . . but . . . a man who can be gentle and sweet . . . like you are. And someone who doesn't run away when you want them. Like being Plato's friend when nobody else liked him. That's being strong.'

The above lines, are lines that were created *on the set*, according to Stern, by James Dean and Natalie Wood. Rewriting is a fact of script-to-movie creation and Stern was hired as a young writer specifically because Stern got along with James Dean. The original screenplay lines for the 'what kind of person do you think a girl wants?' scene are as follows (*note among other changes that this line is omitted*):

Judy, 'Is this what it's like to love somebody?'

Jim, 'You disappointed?'

Judy, (mussing his hair), 'Funny, Jimmy. You're so clean and you – this is silly.'

Jim, 'What?'

Judy, 'You smell like baby powder.'

Jim, 'So do you.'

Judy, 'I never felt so clean before.'

Stern related strongly to Plato, 'I was Plato in many ways, and my wish was to find a Jim Stark who would protect me and teach me' (Nocenti 2000, p. 56). Perhaps this is why James Dean liked Stern. Also, Stern was responsible for the first writings of the tender love scenes between Jim and Judy.

Cohan, in *Masked Men*, will say that Judy provides Jim 'direction for his masculinity' and that she is 'the containing structure for his maturation into a "strong" man himself', and that therefore Jim's acceptance of her 'containing structure' erases the 'bisexuality brought out in his undisguised affection for Plato' (Cohan 1997, p. 153).

I strongly disagree. I think this analysis is only accurate if we cannot see masculinity as an option in 'women', that is, we cannot see the 'butch' in Jim Stark. What Cohan describes is the very foundation of the butch–femme relationship. Because it is a relational construct – a butch is most butch next to a femme, and vice versa, each providing the 'container' for the other's 'different sexual' identity.

I think that in their portrayal of Jim and Judy, James Dean and Natalie Wood are the 1950s' invisible embodiment of the 1990s' able to be seen and visible butch–femme 'couple', as is witnessed in the *Boys Don't Cry* reviews. Judy and Jim are, in their construct of gender, even though it is embodied in a biological male and a female, still 'queer', because it is gendered as butch and femme.

I think this was a conscious construct on their part. When asked if Natalie Wood participated in the improvisational work, Stern replied:

> Natalie and Jim . . . did a lot of investigating – let's try this, let's try that. It shook Hollywood up terribly in the 50's when all the Actors Studio people came out. Their imaginations had been trained to experience their own truth and communicate it to an audience in a surprising way. That's what made Brando so spectacular, and Jimmy too; the choices they made. For instance, I didn't have in the script that Natalie left her compact on that seat in Juvenile Hall.
>
> The payoff comes when Jim hands it to her, in an echo of her handing him the dirt on the bluff, and shows her the mirror and says, 'See the monkey.' I didn't write that. It refers to the monkey he had that night, to her leaving the compact, and finally recognizing that she saw him before. It opens, for her, the possibility of coming to him in the alley. That was the magic of that kind of training. (Nocenti 2000, p. 61)

Judy used her make-up compact throughout the film as a talisman to assure herself of the 'rightness' of her new type of relationship. The device, a 'mirror', is one they can see and then see themselves again in, 're-framing their gaze' as the object passes back and forth between them. They created this device as a symbol for their relationship within the world of the film.

Both script versions of the kiss scene conclude fairly closely to the written lines, which were the following:

> (*Original line*) Jim, 'It's not going to be lonely Judy . . . Not for you and not for me.'
>
> (*Filmed line, note revisions*) Jim, 'Oh . . . wow . . . we're not going to be lonely anymore. Ever. Ever. Not you or me.'
>
> Judy, 'I love somebody. All this time I've been looking for someone to love me and now I love somebody. And it's so easy. Why is it so easy now?'
>
> Jim, 'I don't know. It is for me, too.'
>
> Judy, 'I love you, Jim. I really mean it.' (Stern 1955, p. 48)

After this offering of love, Jim will go out and try to save his friend (Sal Mineo) Plato.

> An officer in the movie, (coincidentally named Ray as in director Nicholas Ray?), asks Dean, 'Things pretty rough for you at home?' As Jim, Dean possibly speaks for all homosexuals when he says, 'If I had one day when I didn't have to be all confused and if I didn't have to feel that I was ashamed of everything . . . if I felt that I belonged some place . . . you know?' (Stern 1955, p. 17)

That need to belong for the butch, the drag queen, the obvious effeminate, or the femme, that is, feminine girl like Judy who wants 'a new kind of man' and so 'settles' for a butch, was such an enormous need in the 1950s that this blatant subculture claimed the only public space available, the gay clubs.

Jim says of Plato's need for himself and Judy, again in a line improvised by Dean, 'He tried to make us his family . . . I guess he wanted us to be . . . his' (Dirks n.d.).

When the police are after Plato, Jim speaks tenderly to a frightened Judy, once again in a sequence completely different from the original screenplay. In the original, Judy does not go with Jim to try to save Plato, but reconciles with her father; in the actor-improvised, filmed version Jim rescues Judy from her father, and they both try to rescue Plato. Judy, fearing for Jim's life, if he tries to rescue Plato, says, 'I need you, too, Jim.' Jim says that Plato needs not only himself Jim, but also needs Judy, too. But in the end Jim and Judy are unable to save him.

It has been said that it was a butch woman who threw the first stone at Stonewall, the gay and lesbian civil rights action in 1969 that sparked the contemporary civil rights movement for homosexual rights in the US. Whether or not this legend is true, butch women were prominently present and they were there protecting a space primarily frequented by drag queens. The people who cleared space, and held space for this community, were its most obvious members – butches, femmes, drag queens, and effeminate men.

In *Rebel* Plato represents the effeminate man – loyal in his portrayal to the extent of keeping a male movie star picture taped in his high school locker. To be his friend requires, as Judy states, a certain bravery. One would have to be brave to be friends with a possibly gay youth in the world of a 1950s US high school. Dean, in being Plato's friend, exemplifies the butch woman's strength to fight for the protection of her community. In fact, the 'castle' that Plato shows Jim, to which Jim later retreats with Judy, could be seen as symbolic of a gay bar which eventually gets 'raided' by homophobic males – as these havens (castles?) of safety and space often actually were in the 1950s.

From an online review of *Rebel*:

> Disenchanted with their own families and removed from the real world, the three teenagers act the part of their own warm, peaceful, idealized family. The young Romeo and Juliet couple wish to explore the mansion further. Before they leave Plato, they put a coat over him . . . They notice . . . red and blue mismatched socks and laugh, 'Must have been a nervous day,' but instead of judging . . . Plato, they identify with his confusion. Jim asks Judy, 'I've done that, though, haven't you?' and she nods. (Dirks n.d.)

Colour in film was relatively new in 1955. While Jim Stark's red jacket has been recognized and I have personally known at least one butch woman who wore a red jacket in imitation of Dean, analysis of this has not previously tied Jim's jacket with Judy's opening costume of red coat, bow tie and lipstick and then tied those with Plato's red sock. Dean on learning the film was to be shot in the new technology technicolour switched his black leather jacket costume for a red windbreaker, and so created a filmic colour to symbolize queerness – and community. In initiating the use of red for this purpose in the film, and aligning the three principles together this way, Dean created what I think in the world of *Rebel* actually looked like the beginning of queer nation.

Plato is roughed up for being queer – one blue sock, one red. Judy is abused by her father; he rubs her red lipsticked lips so hard she says he 'almost rubbed them off'; and we see him slap her. Dean chose the red jacket for his costume. These three instances of obvious red are the only examples of characters wearing red in the film. Why? Yes, it shows their connection to each other, but in connecting it to Plato's mismatched bright red sock, it also shows their allegiance to being 'queer'. 'Different'. Admitting that all three have had 'nervous days'. And I think this was James Dean's intent.

Jim will risk death to enter the planetarium where Plato is locked up. In entering the planetarium with him, Judy embodies the femme lesbian who learns from the butch that she can be strong and a new kind of feminine. A 1950s femme was expected to look the part of a demure, yet sexy and ultimately helpless woman. But, if her girlfriend, or butch, were beaten and raped by the cops many times, she was also prepared to be 'the strong one'.

Images of gay youth were embodied in the actual student body of *Rebel*'s Hollywood High. The butch, the femme and the effeminate teenager – these were the real outsiders at the school that the fictional Judy, Jim and Plato attended. Judy may represent the femme lesbian in love with Jim, the 'as if' butch dyke, and both were friends with the obvious gay boy, Plato.

In making this analysis, I don't want in any way to insinuate that gay men cannot and have not created their own complex yet 'traditional' masculinity. Sal Mineo's personal history illustrates this. He was thrown out of parochial school, and by the age of eight was a member of a street gang in a tough Bronx neighbourhood (<http://www.salmineo.com/>).

In his portrayal of Plato, Mineo utilizes his history, especially in the fight scene with the toughs in the mansion. Again deviating from the original script, he injects his own characterization and brings his own touch to the part. He would also become, as were Dean and Woods already, a method actor. He creates the part in a very different way than would the 'traditional' gay male code of the 1950s. He fights back. He swings a hose at one of the toughs and knocks him into the pool, and shoots and wounds another. He has the gun.

His portrayal might potentially be the subject of an entire study. If he was a known gay male in the film, would he have been allowed to fight back?

He died in the end, perhaps the ultimate result of the Production Code rule, as the necessary punishment of homosexuality. However, the portrayal of an angry dangerous gay male fighting back would not be seen again by the public at large until much later, in the news footage of the Stonewall Inn Riots in 1969.

I don't mean to disregard the undertones of male homo-eroticism in this film. My point is to acknowledge the additional butch–femme dynamic and how that has historically been overlooked.

The Production Code made any reference to homosexuality at all a feat in itself. Stern talks about how at this time any overt reference to homosexuality had to be cut from footage, even the word 'punk' was edited, as it was slang for gay.

This reflects the different codes imposed on TV versus movies. Not that the Production Code was different – but news is news. The Stonewall Inn Riots had to be covered; they were news and had to be televized. Feature films have the burden of how to manipulate the medium so that it will be allowed to film, and to sell, what has not been commercial or allowed. If we read the signs, such as Mineo's transgressive portrayal of a masculine gay youth, or Dean's use of red to symbolize queer community, one cannot help but perhaps admire and speculate as to how the cast and crew of *Rebel* used the feature film medium to transmit a kind of 'news' that was happening, but not yet televised.

This section summarizes my study comparing Dean's other portrayals in *East of Eden* and *Giant*, a commentary on the strong masculine women he is associated with in both films, played by Mercedes McCambridge and Jo Van Fleet.

The canon of Dean films includes some of the only 'trans'-gendered images in the films of the 1950s. Dean was a method actor, one who uses his own emotions and experiences for his work. In all of his movies Dean got to play out the butch persona that he had trouble playing out in real life. Perhaps as a biological male, who was attracted to the same, it was difficult for him to find a partner for that dynamic. Because of stereotypical delineations it is necessary to shake up the limiting paradigms in order to include different combinations of qualities – butch women/butch men, female women/female men – to appreciate the suggested role nuances of the characters Jim and Judy. For example, we have locked butch with female lesbian and strongly effeminate/feminine drag queen with gay men, and so it is hard to visualize the strong femme woman, Judy in *Rebel,* or the butch man, Jim Stark.

In reference to gender coding within homosexual culture, and the personal pressure Dean himself was under, there is a touching scene in Gilmore's *Live Fast and Die Young*. Gilmore describes a night Dean wanted him to dress up as a woman, wearing lace underpants and a biker jacket. In the scene Jimmy lit candles and put Edith Piaf on the record player. Gilmore said he wasn't 'worried about it'. That it didn't seem like it was about him; it was, as Gilmore wrote, something he saw as 'bisexual, and he was the one involving me, coaxing me as it were'. Finally, when the mood was set, Dean orgasmed quickly 'just kissing the legs' of Gilmore. Later in the night Dean went out, got in a fight, came back, and spent a couple of hours in the bathroom alone, and then lay in bed sobbing. Gilmore said he was 'quiet about it, (so) I didn't say anything' (Gilmore 1997, pp. 131–2).

I believe Dean was trying to create a new kind of world where even the usual 'traditional' trans-gressive roles, recognizable homosexual roles that could be played out to a degree in real life, such as those lived by the known homosexuals (known in the world of Hollywood anyway) Rock Hudson and Mercedes McCambridge, didn't work for him. He wanted more fluidity and freedom to be – I believe the word today would be 'queer' – and from all accounts he was very lonely in that desire. Eartha Kitt said, 'he had nobody'.

Dean's friend, the 'butch' Mercedes McCambridge, said, 'I can't tell you how he needed . . . You could feel the loneliness beating out of him, and it hit you like a wave' (Martinetti 1995, p. 147).

In spite of his loneliness, Dean had a gang called The Night Watch. The gang included his male lover(s), the actress Vampira and others who hung out together at a local coffee shop, Googie's. They were 'Jimmy's people', a collection of people who didn't quite fit anywhere. Today we might call them 'queer nation'.

What Dean did and how he did it cannot be separated from, and was commensurate with, the time period in which he lived. During this period details like the mistaken bathroom entry, Plato's male movie star picture, even Plato's wearing of two different colour socks were all signs, daring signs, of 'queerness', and very transgressive for the period.

While it may be true that 'women' and 'men' are signs and we can in an ideal world flow between the two, being able to think about doing that has been fought for. In an ideal world there might be freedom to migrate between the poles of masculinity and femininity without a declaration of allegiance to either. However, without exaggerating, in the 1950s people died for our contemporary right to contemplate 'gender identity'.

Gender identity, how one creates and internalizes one's personal identity, is a basic building block of personality. It is a hard world in which that basic identity is read as transgression.

Unpacking the portrayal of Jim Stark in *Rebel* gives us insight into very thorny contemporary questions. How is humanity defined? What is the role of patriarchal ideology in constructing gender? What is the meaning of liberation in the context of constructed gender?

James Dean can be claimed by homosexual heritage. The 'new man' he personified in *Rebel* can also be claimed in a lineage of butch women. This presents a model for how we look at exclusion/inclusion and how we build community. Reducing the film to the individual male sexual identity or masculine identity formation misses the very real issues of community and/or queer nation, which Ray, Dean, Wood and the rest of the cast and crew struggled to bring forth despite the strict production code of the time.

More work should be done to reframe the gaze around the construction of the fifties 'new man'. This new construction should be based partly on butch identity, and the butch–femme impact on contemporary culture as a whole, its implications within the community itself, and how the community appropriated the screen images of and about itself.

Dean said, 'I think the prime reason for existence, for living in this world, is discovery' (Martinetti 1995, p. 71).

Perhaps it is now time for us to discover exactly what he was exploring.

References

Alexander, Paul (1997), *Boulevard of Broken Dreams: The Life, Times and Legend of James Dean* (New York: Plume).

Bronski, Michael (1984), *Culture Clash: the Making of Gay Sensibility* (Boston, MA: South End Press).

Cartier, Marie (1999), 'Gender Bending and Its Theological Implications within the Canon of James Dean, Particularly in the Film, *Rebel without a Cause*', unpublished paper.

Cohan, Steven (1997), *Masked Men: Masculinity and the Movies in the Fifties* (Bloomington, IN: Indiana University Press).

Dirks, Tim (n.d.), review, *Rebel without a Cause*: <http://www.filmsite.org/rebel.html>.

Gilmore, John (1997), *Live Fast and Die Young: Remembering the Short Life of James Dean* (New York: Thunder's Mouth Press).

Heller, Scott (1999), *The Boston Phoenix*, quoted in *The Los Angeles Times Calendar*, ad for *Boys Don't Cry*, 7 November 1999.

Levy, Emmanuel, '*Boys Don't Cry*: Review', *Variety* 2 September 1999.

Martinetti, Ronald (1995), *The James Dean Story: A Myth-Shattering Biography of a Hollywood Legend* (Secaucus, NJ: Citadel Stars Book).

Nocenti, Annie (2000), 'Writing *Rebel without a Cause*: A Talk with Stewart Stern', *Scenario: The Magazine of Screenwriting Art,* 5.2, p. 56.

Stern, Stewart (1955), *Rebel without a Cause* (screenplay), story: Nicholas Ray, Director: Nicholas Ray (Available from, among others, Script

City, Los Angeles. Also recently published in *Scenario: The Magazine of Screenwriting Art* (1997) 5.2, pp. 10–55).

Villanueva, Chea (1997), 'The Bad Girl', in *Bulletproof Butches* (New York: Masquerade Books), pp. 99–119.

8

The Priest at the Altar: The Eucharistic Erasure of Sex

ELIZABETH STUART

François-Marius Granet's (1775–1849) painting *Priest at the Altar* depicts a priest saying Mass in the traditional eastward-facing position. The priest wears an alb, amice and chasuble and maniple. The alb touches the floor. The priest stands with hands outstretched and head lifted toward heaven. The painting is easily ascribed gender. No doubt Granet was conscious of painting a male priest: there would be no other type of Catholic priest to paint. But what I find striking about this picture is that it is equally easy to gaze upon the priest in such a way as to queer or erase sex. The picture could actually be of a female. Now that those vestments are not associated purely with men, it is possible for us to read the painting in a different manner to previous generations. The vestments and gesture serve to wipe out sex and gender leaving just the human, a human in whom sex is rendered unreadable if it is not simply assumed. This article argues that there is something about the Catholic priesthood in its defining act of celebrating the Eucharist that renders it trans-sexual, that is to say, it demands that sex is taken up into the mystery of redemption where it is erased under a matrix of sacramental signs, symbols and displacements. Sex is placed under Eucharistic erasure and the priest is the central player in that drama.

In Exodus 33 Moses asks the Lord if he may see 'thy glory'. God grants the request while protecting Moses from the fate of one who is exposed to the face of God, namely, death. In order that Moses will not die, God allows him to see his back only (Exod. 33.17–24). For some scholars, such as Howard Eilberg-Schwartz, this exposure of the back of God is a deliberate attempt to obscure the sex of the divine (Eilberg-Schwartz 1997). It allows for metaphors such as Israel being the bride of God to be used without the need to face the unsettling homo-erotic overtones that a clear view of the divine sex would provoke. The sex of God is rendered deliberately ambiguous in this revelation to Moses. The divine will not be sexed.

This use of the back to place sex under such ambiguity that is erased of significance is evident in the Gospel of John's account of the resurrection. Mary stoops to look into the tomb where she finds two angels sitting where the body had lain. She does not understand the significance of their presence, her Lord's absence or their questioning of her mourning. But then she 'turned round and saw Jesus standing, but she did not know it was Jesus'. He asks her the same question as the angels have asked, 'Woman, why are you weeping?' They then have a conversation in which she still fails to recognize the stranger. It is only when he says her name that 'she turned and said to him in Hebrew "Rabboni"' (John 20.11–16). As I have argued elsewhere it is easy for the reader to miss the significance of the second turning here. Mary had already turned away from the tomb towards Jesus when he first appeared, now she turns again away from him so that she now stands with her back towards him (Stuart 2003). In fact, she addresses not the stranger standing behind her but the empty tomb. In the tomb, guarding both the presence and absence of Christ sit the angels. Angels are, of course, sexless. They neither marry nor are given in marriage (Matt. 22.30). They sit recreating the image of the Ark of Covenant (Exod. 25.22), the place of divine/human encounter. It is to this scene that Mary turns in her acknowledgement of Jesus' presence, not to the man. In this act Mary confirms that resurrection erases sex. She turns away from the man and in the process turns away from womanness. This breaking of sex is confirmed by the risen Christ in his command, 'Do not hold me' (John 20.17), better translated 'Do not cleave to me'. The cleaving which is that which holds sex in existence is overturned. No longer need a man leave his father and mother 'and cleave to his wife, and they become one flesh' (Gen. 2.24). Jesus and Mary in this encounter at the tomb deliberately break sex, male and female meet and turn away from each other. Post-resurrection humanity is no longer defined in these terms; the unity of flesh is to be found no longer in sex but in Eucharist, in the union with Christ.

The Eucharist is many things caught up in one action. At its heart is the great mystical transposition of bread and wine into the body and blood of Christ through which the mystery of redemption is once again enacted, stretched through time and space. This action reveals something theologically important about both embodiment and sex. Graham Ward notes that the Gospels portray Jesus' body and gender as unstable from conception and increasingly displaced (Ward 2000, pp. 97–116). In the story of the Last Supper Jesus' body is extended to incorporate bread and wine. Here we can see the beginning of a process of the desexing of Jesus' body. It becomes bread and wine, non-sexed corporeality, able to be ingested in other bodies, becoming one flesh with them. Sex is erased from embodiment. And the unity of the flesh becomes in the Eucharist a union of humanity and embodied divinity.

The understanding of the Eucharist as both a reflection of and participation in the great liturgy of heaven is an ancient one. The book of Revelation describes the heavenly liturgy. Interestingly, this book itself begins with a turn – John 'turns to see the voice' and is immediately plunged into an eschatological dimension which is mirrored in the Eucharist, hence the Orthodox description of the Eucharist as the 'divine liturgy'. The Second Vatican Council emphasized this aspect of the Eucharist:

> [I]n the earthly liturgy we take part in a foretaste of that heavenly liturgy which is celebrated in the holy city of Jerusalem toward which we journey as pilgrims, where Christ is sitting at the right hand of God, a minister of the holies and of the true tabernacle. We sing a hymn to the Lord's glory with all the warriors of the heavenly army. Venerating the memory of the saints, we hope for some part and fellowship with them. We eagerly await the Saviour, our Lord Jesus Christ, until He, our life, shall appear and we too will appear with Him in glory. (*Sacrosanctum concilium* 8)

The heavenly liturgy as described in the book of Revelation focuses not on a chalice and host but on the sacrificial lamb. The displacement of one-fleshness from marriage to Eucharist is evidenced in that liturgy being designated 'the marriage feast of the Lamb' in Revelation 19.9. In the figure of the Lamb Christ is rendered once again sexless, embodied but no longer purely human. He becomes a cosmic figure. The marriage between him and his Church is one which further erases sex. For his 'bride' is not one sex just as is it not one nationality, race or class. Indeed, it is not just one human state, consisting as it does of the living and the dead. The Bride is multi-sexed, multi-social, national and cultural and multi-dimensional, the many undermining the reality of the one. Dualism and divisions are dissolved and in the process the thickness of these categories is dissipated to the point of nothingness so that the Bride, like the Lamb, emerges from the tomb of sex as something different.

The anticipatory nature of the Eucharist was emphasized by Pope John Paul II:

> The Eucharist is a straining towards the goal, a foretaste of the fullness of joy promised by Christ (cf. Jn 15:11); it is in some way the anticipation of heaven, the 'pledge of future glory' . . . The eschatological tension kindled by the Eucharist *expresses and reinforces our communion with the Church in heaven.* It is not by chance that the Eastern Anaphoras and the Latin Eucharistic Prayers honour Mary, the ever-Virgin Mother of Jesus Christ our Lord and God, the angels, the holy apostles, the glorious martyrs and all the saints. This is an aspect of the Eucharist which merits greater attention: in celebrating the sacrifice of the Lamb, we are united to the heavenly 'liturgy' and become part of that great multitude which cries out: 'Salvation belongs to our God who sits upon the throne, and to the Lamb!' (Rev 7:10). The Eucharist is truly a glimpse of heaven appearing on earth. It is a glorious ray of the heavenly Jerusalem which pierces the clouds of our history and lights up our journey. (John Paul II 2003, 18 and 19)

In the Eucharist we participate in what John Paul II called the 'secret' of resurrection. We enter the liminal space between what is and what is to come, the entrance to the tomb, the edge of heaven. It is a space of turning. Judith Butler has identified 'the turn' as a key to the emergence of the subject. The subject either turns to authority or to the self in a turning-in upon oneself which is bound up with melancholy and grief which, for Butler, is the root of gender (Butler 1997). The Eucharistic turn cuts a swathe through all this. The turn towards the heavenly Jerusalem is, as Mary Magdalene demonstrates, precisely a turn away from sex, from melancholy and from earthly authority. It is a turn which represents the end of sex.

The priest is the one who stands on the cutting edge of heaven. In the celebration of the Eucharist (particularly if celebrated *ad orientem*) the priest leads the Church away from a world of male and female towards the divine world in which subjectivity is defined purely in terms of union with God. The priest is the one who enables the Church to experience that union, the marriage with the Lamb through the consumption of the body and blood of Christ. As the person at the front line of the Eucharistic action, it is imperative that the priest embodies the end of sex. This is much harder hard to do in a celebration of the Eucharist *contra populum* where the priest is positioned physically as a mediator between people and divinity and the sex of the priest is evident for all to see. But vestments veil the sex of the priest and also serve to remind those present that the priest is not there as an individual but represents another. Exactly what Other the priest represents continues the process of queering the priesthood and Church.

Traditionally, of course, the priest is understood to stand in *persona Christi* and it is around this concept that so much of the discussion over the ordination of women has revolved. But, as Graham Ward has noted, it is a categorical theological mistake to think that acting *in persona Christi* is about performing maleness. From the moment of his conception Jesus is caught up in a divine queering of sex. He is a male born of no male matter, the result of an overshadowing by the Holy Spirit, a manifestation of the Shekinah, the presence of the divine understood in Judaism to be the female manifestation of God's presence which overshadowed the Ark of the Covenant and the Temple. The sacrifice of the Eucharist which is enacted by the priest acting in *persona Christi* is to some extent a sacrifice of sex. When the priest performs the consecration and utters the words, 'This is my body . . . This is my blood' s/he gazes at a piece of bread and a cup of wine, at an embodiment made strange and sexless. This is the Christ but it is also the priest. And it is also the Church which through the act of communion becomes the Body of Christ.

As well as standing *in persona Christi* the priest stands *in persona Ecclesiae*, the post-Ascension body of Christ made up of a multitude of sexes, genders, races, classes, nationalities and so on. The priest leads and represents the Church before the throne of God. Incorporation into this body through baptism involves the decentralizing of all defining classifications as the ancient baptismal formula cited by St Paul in Galatians 3.28 makes clear. In Christ there is no male and female. The ancient rite of the blessing of the baptismal waters at the Easter Vigil speaks of the font as a womb through which human beings are 'born again as new creatures . . . a heavenly offspring . . . that all who are distinguished either by sex in body or by age in time, may be brought forth to the same infancy by grace, their mother'. Into the font are plunged sex and age and what emerges is a new creation, the product of the resurrection. It is this new creation which the priest represents before God, a sexless humanity, a humanity looking into the tomb living on transformed bread and wine. This is humanity whose identity is erased by the very excess of it. No one is excluded and the act of inclusion obliterates identity which is always predicated upon exclusion.

The Eucharist is a re-enactment of the great drama of salvation. The consecration of the bread and wine makes Christ as truly present as he was in a stable in Bethlehem or on a cross on Calvary. The priest may then be understood as a midwife facilitating the bringing forth of the Christ or indeed as a mother birthing through his/her body the great miracle of salvation. In this regard then the priest could be said to be standing in the person of Mary. If Christ has long been understood as the great High Priest of redemption, there is also a parallel tradition of understanding the Blessed Virgin Mary as a priest. Mary was widely believed to be of priestly descent. St Andrew of Crete was one of a number of early Church theologians who describe Mary as being descended from the priesthood of Aaron (Andrew of Crete, *First Homily on the Nativity*, para. 96). She is variously described in early Christian theology as the Ark, the Holy of Holies, the altar and the priestly staff but also more explicitly as priest. Epiphanius described her as 'both priest and altar' (Epiphanius, *De Laudibus Virginis*, para. 49). Theodore Studites hails the Blessed Virgin as 'the young sacrificial priest' (Theodore Studites, Cant. 7.1) As time moves on the ascription of priesthood to Mary becomes more common. Albert the Great in the thirteenth century argued that Mary possessed priesthood 'equivalently and eminently' to those in Holy Orders.[1] It was in the seventeenth century that the priestly role and nature of Mary was discussed in most detail and depth. Jacques de Vasseur was among a number of theologians who at this time attributed to Mary the role of bishop and sacrificing priest (Jacques de Vasseur, *Diva Virgo*, ch. 22). In the nineteenth century several theologians took the view that is it highly significant that the mother of Christ was said by the Gospels to have *stood* at the foot of cross. The physical stance was significant because it was the position of a sacrificing priest. Cardinal Laplace put it thus: 'Mary on Calvary stood erect, as a sacrificer, as a priest at the altar, *Virgo Sacerdos*, offering in her heart the Victim of the world' (Laplace 1884, p. 13). And J. M. Raynaud argued,

> Mary stands upright. Why? . . . There is a mystery here. It is that Mary is not only witness to Jesus' death. She is also priest, the first to offer the divine victim who sacrifices himself for us. The cross, well, it is the altar. Jesus, well, he is the victim. Do not search for the priest. It is Mary![2]

Devotion to Mary, the Virgin Priest, was widespread and encouraged in nineteenth-century Roman Catholicism but brought to an abrupt end in the twentieth century with papal bans first on images depicting Mary as priest and then on devotions to her in this capacity.[3] Throughout Christian history Mary has sometimes been depicted in art as bishop

1 *B. Alberti Magni, Ratisbonensis Episcopi, Ordinis Praedicatorum, Opera Omnia*, ed. Augustus and Aemilius Borgnet (Paris 1890–9), vol. 37, pp. 62–246.

2 Raynaud 1843, vol. 2, pp. 251–2.

3 <http://www.womenpriests.org/mrpriest/mpr_ovr.asp>.

(wearing the *pallium*) or in priestly vestments, perhaps most strikingly in the fifteenth-century *Le sacerdoce de la Vierge* by an unknown French artist, where she clearly wears a chasuble and stole standing before an altar and holding a paten.[4]

If the Virgin Mary may be understood to be a priest, perhaps the prototypical priest because she was the first to be able to say, 'This is my body, this is my blood', and to offer it as a sacrifice then the priest celebrating Mass may be understood to stand in the person of Mary as much as Christ. So the priest standing before the altar stands in the person of Christ whose sex was destabilized from the moment of conception, the Church which is multi-sexed and Mary the Virgin priest whose priesthood defies the sexual conventions of the ages in which she is so described. The priest then offering a sacrifice in the non-sexed form of bread and wine is a transsexual figure representing the theo-ontological status of the baptized who are led by the priest into the meta-reality of divine life through the communion of one-fleshness with the Christ who is an extension of incorporation into that life at baptism. At baptism the believer is integrated into the Body of Christ which is bread and wine, which is Lamb, which is the Church, which is the historical Jesus but which is never straightforwardly sexed. The Eucharist is the space in which sex is erased and that erasure is enacted by the priest on behalf of the people. The priest him/herself at ordination further extends the baptismal identity into a deeper eschatological space. The priest is set apart sacramentally to stand between worlds, to be the embodiment of a world being born in another, a world of non-sex being birthed into a world of sex, a world in which no other identity except that of Christ has ultimate concern, being birthed into a world in which humans divide from each other by identity constructions.

This set apartness is evident in the celebration of the sacraments but in Catholic tradition carries through into the everyday life of the priest in terms of dress and celibacy. The Catholic priest then is a transsexual, one who transcends sex by containing and representing both sex made complex as represented by Christ and Mary and an excess of sex represented

4 <http://www.womenpriests.org/mrpriest/gallery2.asp>.

by the multitudinous sex of the Church, to the point of obliteration. By standing with back to the people the priest embodies, anticipates and leads into a divine life beyond sex.

All this is beautifully illustrated in the works of the contemporary British mystic, Elizabeth Wang. Wang is a Roman Catholic with conservative views on matters theological and would not agree with my reading of the priesthood and Mass. Wang has produced a series of paintings which depict the mystic dimensions of the Mass.[5] The Mass she paints is the post-Vatican II rite celebrated *contra populum*. Wang is opposed to the ordination of women. Yet the images she paints always depict the sex of the priest and all those involved in the Mass as erased. What erases the identity of the participants are the explosions of glory (remember the back of God in Exod. 33) which she illustrates blasting through at key points of the liturgy, drawing all participants into itself and in the process erasing all identity in a flare of colour. The figure of the Christ, also rendered sexless, overshadows the priest, each the shadow of the other while, as the canon begins, Mary and John appear at the side of the altar standing at the foot of the cross which stretches itself through eternity, though we only know who these figures are by virtue of their position and Wang's commentary, for they too are sexless figures (Wang 2001, pp. 16–17). Wang sees the Eucharist becoming more populated as earth and heaven meet in one liturgical celebration: angels, saints and the departed become part of the scene until at communion millions of beings are present in one great celebration, gathered around the altar. None reveals sex. Wang's paintings reveal clearly why this is so. The great explosions of divine in the liturgy are intensely desirable; they depict an erotic transcendence which stirs longing for the end of desire itself in the eternal divine. The Eucharist enacts the end of sex because it offers the fulfilment of desire. We consume the beloved in the conscious act of receiving communion, but what the mystical insight reveals is that the beloved also consumes us with his glory. And this mutual consummation is the marriage of the Lamb. When the celebration of the Eucharist directs desire by choreographing the gaze of participants away from the

5 <http://www.radiantlight.org.uk/art_gallery_mass_beginning_end.php>.

divine and onto human interaction, the radical, political and transformative nature of the Eucharist is in danger of being lost on the participants, rather like being at your own wedding but not engaging with the one you have come to marry. The mystical dimension to the Eucharist is essential to understanding its radical nature when it comes to sex.

What the Eucharist reveals is that, for the baptized, sex, gender, sexuality and all other forms of identity by which humans categorize themselves are not of ultimate concern. When they are treated as such, forces of spiritual entropy are unleashed as they are whenever idolatry is practised, and this has been patently evident in recent ecclesiastical discussions on matters of sexuality and gender. We create cultures and ways of living which the Holy Spirit works through and blows through seeking to transform, and until the divine liturgy is realized in time and space we have to live within these constructions, but the Eucharist provides an eschatological space in which those constructions are both present and transcended. It then provides a model for prophetic Christian living.

Such prophetic living requires living sex in such a way that it is evidentially non-ultimate and waiting erasure. There can therefore be no place in Christian living for a sexual hierarchy of any sort in any aspect of life. It is also essential that the Christian community is one in which there is a multiplicity of sexual identities represented and celebrated because the very excess of such identities points towards erasure. The celibate lifestyle must be honoured as an embodied reminder of the fact that all desire ultimately ends in one-fleshness with the divine. The transsexual person must be welcomed and honoured as someone who embodies the instability of sex and gender. However, the Eucharistic theology of erasure demands something of the Christian transsexual. It requires of the transsexual that they accept that the sex they feel more comfortable in is itself not stable or thick with reality. It is not their ultimate identity, only an identity of the second order and it itself has to be performed subversively to expose its non-ultimacy. The transsexual along with every other Christian is obliged to perform their sex in such a way as to reveal its Eucharistic erasure which means resisting the gender scripts which society teaches us through performance. This is a particularly difficult demand for the transsexuals who yearn to differentiate themselves from one sex and to embed themselves in another. This reminds us of another difficult truth taught by the Eucharist, namely, that love is sacrifice and the desire that propels us towards one-fleshness with the divine is about the destruction of the self – the breaking and consumption of a body. Eucharistic erasure is never a painless process because sacrifice is its shape and rhythm. Living in the reality of the Eucharist demands a counter-cultural performance of identity which demands effort, endurance and courage. The priest is one called to embody that performance with no respite, sacrificing in their own person for all their life the sex that gives meaning in contemporary culture. Priesthood begins to lose much of its meaning when the Church forgets the Eucharistic theology of sexuality and buys into constructions of personhood which render sex as stable, thick and truthful. In the past this has led to the maleness of the priest being subject to theological fetishization and sex being given ultimate status. Now that the notion of male superiority has been challenged and the priest may often not be male the power of sex lies more in sexuality and its expression. The priest then becomes an anomaly in both culture and the ecclesiastical system and vulnerable to being rendered valueless. Priests themselves desire to be sexed to be given meaning and to make sense in a sexed world and are reluctant to wear the clothes, the vestments and the habits of priesthood. The value of a celibate life is questioned. Love is no longer understood to be sacrifice but the mutual fulfilling of desire. It is into this our present reality that the Eucharist explodes, demanding that we turn towards a different horizon, the horizon of heaven.

References

Butler, Judith (1997), *The Psychic Life of Power: Theories in Subjection* (Stanford: Stanford University Press).

Eilberg-Schwartz, Howard (1997), 'The Problem of the Body for the People of the Book', in Timothy K. Beal and David M. Gunn, eds, *Reading Bodies, Writing Bodies* (London: Routledge), pp. 34–55.

Laplace, Cardinal L. (1884), *Marie, mère des graces* (Rennes).

John Paul II (2003), *Ecclesia De Eucharista* (Rome: Vatican).
J. M. Raynaud (1843), *Marie modèle. Station du mois de Mai* (Toulouse).
Stuart, Elizabeth (2003), 'Towards the Tomb: Priesthood and Gender', *Theology and Sexuality* 10.1, pp. 30–9.
Wang, Elizabeth (2001), *The Majesty of the Mass* (Harpenden: Radiant Light).
Ward, Graham (2000), *Cities of God* (London and New York: Routledge).

9

Action and Reflection: One Pastor's Method of Creating Trans Day of Remembrance Liturgy

MALCOLM HIMSCHOOT

Transgender lives are rich in theological dimension. As a female-to-male transsexual man and a minister I am grateful that published theological reflection is beginning to register trans perspectives – perspectives that lead into deeper understanding of themes such as embodiment, relationality, following Jesus and being part of God's creation and ongoing new creation. Theological beliefs, by themselves, are one part of the fabric of faith. Action is another. In the spirit of liberation theology's *orthopraxy*, or concern for right action,[1] I offer a situational liturgy for churches whose awareness of the suffering of transgender people is increasing, who find themselves recognizing each November the international Transgender Day of Remembrance (TDOR) – a grassroots event organized by transgender leaders and identified as an important mode of organizing toward visibility, power and human rights.

Transgender Day of Remembrance exists in a context of trauma, amidst which people hold candlelight vigils and participate in a ritual calling out the names of people who recently died brutally violent, anti-

---

1 Action-and-reflection methodology is distilled from various liberation theologies. Letty Russell uses 'praxis' or 'practical theology' to speak of the inductive movement between thinking about Christ's way and acting in solidarity, which was Christ's way. Letty Russell (1974), *Human Liberation in a Feminist Perspective: A Theology* (Philadelphia: Westminster Press), p. 55.

transgender deaths, oppression against the gender-variant targets, both the dead and the living. In awareness of their commonality, despite their different social locations and various different levels of privilege, the living pledge to honour the dead and to strive for 'never again'. Sometimes clergy are involved in Transgender Day of Remembrance. The ceremony may even be held in a church.[2] Liturgy for the community to read aloud together presents an opportunity for theology to occupy not just a theoretical or derivative place in textbooks, but also a place of connection to people's real lives. Core hopes and dilemmas of the community find expression, and in recognition of their challenges the community embraces sacred tasks of creative memory and courageous determination. Theology is tested and reformed in such a place, even as theology motivates action toward social change.

The spiritual work facing transgender people is nothing more and nothing less than the task of faith in every generation. It was first the task of the Israelites upon being led forth into the Promised Land (Josh. 4.1–8). As the Israelites crossed over the Jordan, they were asked to pick up stones from the middle of the river. These stones would become a monument on the other side. What stones would they pick up, in order to memorialize their experience of bondage? Could they truly lay down these same stones, and continue moving past that mile-marker to a new experience? Each stone undoubtedly carried the weight of loss, the mourning and guilt felt for non-survivors. The need for their names and stories to be retold could not be denied, and so it became ritualized in the annual Passover tradition. Neither could the anger at such long subjugation be neglected, and so it was liturgized in psalms that became part of the canon of both Jews and Christians. Neither could the fear be buried,

---

2 In Denver, Colorado, not known for a huge trans population, a 2008 TDOR ceremony memorialized not one but two Coloradoan women killed the preceding year – Angie Zapata and Aimee Wilcoxson. One of the women had supportive family members in the area who were grateful for the outreach and support of the transgender community. The TDOR memorial service that year was trilingual (Spanish – English – American Sign Language) and included my participation as a Protestant, as well as participants who were Catholic, Unitarian Universalist, Ifa, Protestant, Evangelical, Buddhist, Jewish and Native American.

a basic acknowledgement of the contingency of life, the fact that if this savage injustice happened once it could happen again. Dealing with the *loss*, *anger* and *fear* related to secondary trauma is a daunting challenge but a crucial opportunity when creating liturgy for the Transgender Day of Remembrance. I decided to work with those pastoral themes by carrying on in liturgy a scriptural dialogue between lament and proclamation, pain and promise, grief and hope.

Anger is where the liturgy starts: anger as communally expressed in the words of certain psalms. Anger at God, certainly. Many theologians (the Bible's Job among them) have explained why it is appropriate to direct such an expression to God. We feel it; God can handle it. Frustration, entreaty, longing, rage, are all human emotions found present in the psalms, and found unresolved there – as but one part of a dialogue with a living entity on the other side. It is possible, however, that anger in the text is not only *to* God but also *from* God in the way that all good gifts are from God. Anger is an important part of the motive for transformation of injustice. As Augustine of Hippo said, or at least is quoted as saying on a refrigerator magnet in my home, 'Hope has two beautiful daughters. Their names are anger and courage; anger at the way things are, and courage to see that they do not remain the way they are.' Without allowing ourselves to feel anger, we can too easily become mollified, complacent and complicit – no matter if Lazarus is lying in torment near us, or if dams to the river of life are built up all around us, or if bad fruit is taking root within us. Anger is a healthy indicator of all these dysfunctions. Giving anger a place in liturgy, without sanitizing it or asking it to go away, is worthwhile. It names the need for liberation, and calls God to account for promises to be with the oppressed, when the very God who promised seems absent.

Fear is not the same as anger, and needs its own response. Theologically, fear cannot be answered with violent triumphalism, although this is one option that various Scriptures present. *If the memory of the past is defeat and injury, the promise of the future is to vanquish our enemies*! In truth, fear that seeks safety in violence only begets more fear and more violence and more fear in a contagious and escalating cycle. Based on grief, fear is an emotion that fundamentally needs comfort. Comfort can be sought via denial of a traumatic reality, but it can also be sought in courageous resistance to an unjust reality. In Jesus' teachings I find the latter: love (the verb) as a clear alternative to fear, a reclamation of a reality more true and honorable, more just and pure, more pleasing, excellent, commendable and praiseworthy than any tale told by violence. Jesus bequeaths an ontological story of experientially engaging suffering in order to transform it. It is a story of present and future comfort, especially for those most affected by unjust suffering. For that reason my liturgy departs from the psalms and instead draws on the words of Jesus in the Matthean Beatitudes. The Beatitudes are full of paradoxes, capable of offering comfort and kindling resistance at the same time. Of course Jesus' words have been preached often by the powerful as passive placebo only, but in context they have been well understood by many people as compassionate transformation of the status quo.[3]

As for loss, words fail. And so we need silence. It could be a very effective Trans Day of Remembrance ceremony that took place entirely in silence. My liturgy includes only two small portions of silence. It errs, as most Protestant traditions do, on the side of using words to cover the distance between people. At least the liturgy reaches its limit when Scripture does, when the biblical texts become completely metaphorical, pointing to the hope beyond death, when both Jesus' teaching and the final passage from psalms mention the phrase 'child/ren of God'. I do not fully know what that means. Maybe it means, to the grieving mother, friends, siblings, 'We recognize their wholeness and the mystery of their wholeness. Dead or alive, all the earth belongs to them, just as they belong to the earth.' Maybe it means, 'Their divine inheritance is untouched – from Spirit they have returned to Spirit.' Maybe it means, 'Jesus their brother is dining with them in paradise.' I do not know the extent of the theol-

3 Theology of nonviolence does not always meet theology of liberation, but I find promising contemporary trajectories in the work of Jack Nelson-Pallmeyer, J. Denny Weaver and Dorothee Sölle. The secular journalist Mark Kurlansky in his 2006 book *Nonviolence: Twenty-Five Lessons from the History of a Dangerous Idea*, New York: Modern Library, notes that the lack of a noun, other than 'pacifism', for what Jesus promoted leaves him open to misunderstanding. Nonviolence is a better word if it connotes active engagement.

ogy that can come from these words. I simply know that by action, when a community gathers and mourns, when those who are feeling strong touch those who are feeling weak, when candles are lit and the presence of God is invoked, when the mystery of theodicy is summoned in anger and fear and sadness, when life and death are recognized as sacred, when murder is denied the last word, then the way forward together becomes a little more fathomable. The way of hope and liberation.

Transgender Day of Remembrance is a promising point on which to locate religious action and reflection. Yet it carries a problematical tension, having to do with the impact of secondary trauma. As much as we experience shock and rage over one death, as much as we say, 'Never again', everybody who has been keeping track of Transgender Day of Remembrance (now in its eleventh year) knows that incidents of hate, bias and violence will happen again. In fact we plan ahead ways of keeping track and registering where and to whom they will happen. In a population with disproportionately high rates of attempted or committed suicide, it could be that the internalization of dead-end possibilities is one risk to making such remembrance a key focus for organizing toward empowerment. We who are still living can too easily psychologically project ourselves into a position of victimization and anticipation of death. The side effects are not very liberating. They can lead to the opposite of wholeness if we close off, get stuck, or lash out – all of which are understandable reactions to trauma, but not beneficial for living generous and justice-seeking lives.

Side effects such as reinforced feelings of anxiety and harm for transgender people, along with the limitation for mainstream communities of reducing transgender people to objects of pity, have raised the issue whether it would not be better to concentrate on a different occasion for transgender visibility. There is logic to this, and so now there is also a Transgender Day of Empowerment (5 April) in addition to a Transgender Day of Remembrance (20 November). Community members concentrate on pride, survival and progress in unique ways.

Yet, hate crimes persist in great numbers, and many trans people are not far from someone who is victimized each year. To go through the year without acknowledging forces that often manifest as violence but which also manifest as alienation, isolation, marginalization, domination, assimilation, discrimination and exploitation, leaves the transgender community without grounding in part of our real historical context. It makes invisible, and thus more powerful, the forces at work against us all, whether we acknowledge them or not. A further argument for continuing Day of Remembrance is to gain traction on interlocking oppressions such as racism and classism – since street violence is inflicted more often on low-income (trans) women of colour than on elite white members of the trans community. Transgender Day of Remembrance offers a tool for collective knowledge and grounding in our shared context. Painful as it is, it can be done in a manner that raises leadership, that raises our collective sights, and that raises alternative consciousness. Says Michelle O'Brien, activist in Philadelphia:

> In the midst of this horror, finding ways of coming to terms with our loss, healing from our pain and treasuring our lives and the lives of others couldn't be more urgent or necessary. At the heart of revolutionary struggle and liberation is the understanding that each person is precious and valuable, that oppression must end precisely because it denies people the means of fully expressing and fulfilling our rich possibilities of beauty, love and compassion.[4]

Liturgy that addresses the themes of pain and possibility, horror and hope, is not only a work of theological reflection but a work of action, done by a community together. Such action, God willing, can inform theology just as theology can inform future action.

---

4 Michelle O'Brien, 2004, 'Mourning Our Dead, Demanding Our Lives', <http://www.deadletters.biz/ourdead.html>.

For F. C. Martinez and Angie Zapata

LAMENT AND PROCLAMATION

For use by communities during Transgender Day of Remembrance, a commemoration of lives lost worldwide to violence against gender-nonconforming people.

Reader 1:

How long, O God?

How long will transgender people suffer shame and loss because of who we are?

How long must we bear pain in our souls, and have sorrow in our hearts all day long?

How long shall we have enemies who persecute us, ridicule us, and gloat over us?
(*adapted from Psalm 10*)

Reader 2:

Consider and answer me, O Lord my God!

Give light to my eyes, or I will sleep the sleep of death,

And my enemy will say, 'I have prevailed.'

(*from Psalm 13*)

Reader 3:

Why do you stand far off, hiding yourself in times of trouble?

In fear the violent attack the vulnerable –

Let them be caught in the schemes their hearts have devised.

In confusion and disturbance the oppressors say,

'There is no God who cares for the meek –

No God will find me out.'

Their mouths are filled with cursing and deceit and oppression

They sit in ambush

In stealth they murder the innocent.

The helpless fall by their might.

They think:

'God has forgotten [the drag queens and cross-dressers, transgender men, transgender women, transgender children and youth, gender-queer people and intersex individuals]* –

God has hidden God's face.'

Rise up, O Lord; O God, lift up your hand

Do not forget the oppressed.
(*from Psalm 10*)

Silence

READER 4: Matthew 5.1–9

When Jesus saw the crowds, he went up the mountain; and after he sat down, his disciples came to him. Then he began to speak, and taught them, saying:

'Blessed are the poor in spirit, for theirs is the kingdom of heaven.

'Blessed are those who mourn, for they will be comforted.

'Blessed are the meek, for they will inherit the earth.

'Blessed are those who hunger and thirst for righteousness, for they will be filled.

---

* In this line place whatever names and identities best affirm the community.

'Blessed are the merciful, for they will receive mercy.

'Blessed are the pure in heart, for they will see God.

'Blessed are the peacemakers, for they will be called children of God.'

Silence

All Gathered:

Why do murderers rage, and fearful people plot in vain?
Those in power, and those who long for power, conspire
Against the precious anointed of the Lord.
In heaven God laughs at their presumption.

I will tell of the decree of the Living, Mighty God
Who said to me, 'You are my child. Today I have begotten you.
Ask of me, and I will make the earth itself your inheritance.'
(*from Psalm 2*)

Note: *Lament and Proclamation* appears courtesy of the United Church of Christ Office for Health, Wholeness, and Lesbian, Gay, Bisexual and Transgender Ministry, whose website first encouraged congregations to make use of this resource.

10

Towards a Transgender Theology: Que(e)rying the Eunuchs

LEWIS REAY

> Queer theology is, then, a first person theology: diasporic, self-disclosing, autobiographical and responsible for its own words. (Althaus-Reid 2003, p. 8)

> And then there are eunuchs. We find them in the streets, carrying messages, escorting wealthy women, guarding young children. They are beardless, carefully groomed, well dressed in expensive clothing, for they are the costly, elite agents and servants, the elegant adornments of a wealthy, urban, aristocracy. (Ringrose 2003, p. 1)

Introduction

A diasporic, self-disclosing autobiographical narrative is what you will find here. The story of how eunuchs came to find each other in the pages of Scripture; in an upstairs room above a seedy bar in King's Cross; in a sex club in San Francisco; in Metropolitan Community Churches the world over. This is the story of a community coming together to self-knowledge, to autonomy, to visibility and to existence. This is the story of eunuchs, long dead, and the story of transgender people, alive and kicking, and finding our God-given gender identity.

The Much-Overlooked Eunuch

Biblical eunuchs have been much overlooked, though they appear throughout the Bible in a variety of (dis)guises, easily overlooked, but playing significant roles in the unfolding story of God's relationship with humankind. The Ethiopian Eunuch is our most famous *transcestor*.[1] However, there are many others scattered throughout the Bible, both visible and invisible. We shall meet some of these characters later.

First, I wish to consider Jesus' extraordinary saying in Matthew 19 about different types of eunuchs.

> Not everyone can accept this teaching, but only those for whom it is meant. For there are eunuchs who were born that way, and there are eunuchs who have been made so by others, and there are those who have made themselves eunuchs because of the rule of heaven. Let anyone receive this message who can. (Matt. 19.11–12, as translated in Bohache 2006, p. 509).

To my transgender ears and eyes the meaning of this text is plain. Not so however, to generations of biblical scholars. These verses have traditionally been interpreted to suggest that some are called to a celibate life, or that marriage is not for everyone, especially if their calling is of greater importance (Moxnes 2003). More recently queer theologians have used these verses to support the radical inclusion of sexual minorities, such as gay and lesbian people (Bohache 2006; Moxnes 2003; Wilson 1995). Indeed, in the context of the previous verses where Jesus is discussing marriage and divorce it appears logical to consider those who are sexually disenfranchised by the heterosexual patriarchal hegemony. In taking the reading of this text further, I would not wish to suggest that these readings are invalid, rather that the text also supports another equally valid reading.

1 I coin this term *transcestor* as the elision of trans and ancestor to signify those transgender characters and people who provide a history and prove that we have always been here. It was first coined for me by a young transman to whom I am indebted.

I would suggest that the Matthew 19 verses are the clearest statement that Jesus makes about the inclusivity of the new realm. This is a realm where no one is excluded, even the most marginal outsider. Jesus proposes to turn the social order quite literally outside in.

The Greek word *eunoucoi* comes from the root *eune,* a bed, and the verb *echein*, to hold: thus a *eunuch* is a 'bed-keeper' or more literally a 'bed-companion' or 'chamberlain' who was responsible for taking care of a monarch's numerous wives. It also appears as 'court official' or just 'official'. The secondary meaning of the word is an emasculated man, or one naturally incapacitated from marriage, or having children, or one who voluntarily abstains from marriage.

In the Old Testament, the Hebrew word *çârîyç* or *saris* means 'to castrate'; it also means a eunuch or an official. The word appears 13 times translated as 'chamberlain', 17 times as 'eunuch' and 12 times as 'officer' (Strong 2001, p. 691). The word *rabçârîyç* or *rabsaris* appears 3 times meaning 'chief chamberlain' and is used to describe a Babylonian official (Strong 2001, p. 805).

The three categories of eunuchs that Jesus describes are those 'born that way' or literally 'out of the mother's womb' or, possibly, 'out of the inner most part of a man, the soul or heart'; second, those 'made so by others'; and third, those 'who have made themselves eunuchs for the sake of the rule of heaven'. The parallel that I would draw is to those born intersex, those who are transgender in the broadest sense of this word and, third, those who are gender different, or gender queer, that is, not conforming to normative definitions of gender roles and identities. This broad understanding of the Matthew 19 verses, therefore, includes all those marginalized by virtue of their gender expression.

Meet the Family

Let me introduce you to some of my spiritual transcestors – Carcas, the severe, Mehuman, the faithful, Hegai, the eunuch, Zethar, the star, Harbona, the ass-driver, Abagtha, the God-given, and Biztha, the booty, all eunuchs of King Xerxes (see the book of Esther).

Ebed-melech, the servant of the king, an Ethiopian eunuch in the service of King Zedekiah, through whose interference Jeremiah was released from prison; Ashpenaz, the chief eunuch of Nebuchanezzar, Teresh, the strict, who plotted to kill King Xerxes, Sarsechim, the prince among eunuchs, and Shaashgaz, the servant of the beautiful.

Meet some *rabsaris*, chief eunuchs and high-ranking Babylonian officials: Hatach, the truthful, Bigthan, the juicy, and Bigtha, the juiciest.

And, not least, the famous Daniel, and his three friends Hananiah, Mishael and Azariah and the defiant Meshach, Shadrach and Abednego (see the book of Daniel). Finally, our Ethiopian cousin, from Acts, who opens up the possibility of full inclusion into Jesus' new realm to all, not simply the Jewish world.

I am from these, powerful gender-variant souls, whose line stretches throughout history. It can, to my mind, only be described as a movement of the Spirit, that in the mid-1990s, female-to-male identified people started coming out in their droves, across the world. Individual trailblazers made documentaries, appeared on television, in books, and on the radio, and others saw them. As a wave of unknowingly Spirit-led artists and otherwise deviant souls felt the calling of their ancestors and communities of female-bodied, male-gendered men appeared, shorter and gentler than their taller more dominant cousins. I am one of these men. We began to find ourselves and each other in an upper room, gathered around a table, not sharing communion, but building community, in the way that many female-bodied activists have done for generations. We come from a long line of difficult vocal souls. We organized, we talked, we cared, we shared stories, we lobbied, we came out, we cut our hair, and let our beards grow as the hormones we took began their work. We were born again, into male forms, and the world began to take notice.

Many were rejected, some of us lost our minds for a little while, and some of us lost our jobs and our lovers and our families. Many of us felt the Spirit calling and began to find our roots in ancient shamans and forgotten healers, people who had lived in-between and in the shoreline where genders meet. We carved out places where we could exist; we changed our bodies to make them fit as best we could. We discovered that we have always been here, always in the shadows, always being born, some with obvious bodies, some hidden – we are the passing women, the tomboys, two-spirit, amazons, *hijra* and drag kings. We have been kings, popes, soldiers, doctors, musicians, activists (Feinberg 1996). Often undiscovered, until we lie upon the mortuary slab, our gender contradictions exposed for all to finally see, as our bodies declare the hidden truths.

Out of the Inner-Most Part

The invisibility of intersex and transgender people throughout history requires detective work and the ability to see beneath the text to draw out the inevitability of gender-variant queer people in historical biblical accounts. We have always been here, so why should it not be so. Our eunuchs, *saris*, *eunoucoi*, intersex, transgender, *hijra,* third sex, two-spirit, gender-queer heroes and sheroes are our people. They are proof enough of a history of gender-variant people woven into the thread of the text. Not only this, many are named in the ancient Hebrew text as we saw above.

The (dis)appearance of intersex and transgender people throughout history is indicative of the 'subjugated knowledge' (Foucault 1980) that our very existence represents. Goss suggests that 'Subjugated knowledges possess a memory of exclusion, resistance, and struggle in relation to dominant discourses and institutional practices' (Goss 1993, p. 183). The natural diversity of physical genders has been systematically eradicated, such that the dualist worldview of male and female renders biological fact invisible. In truth, human beings come in a variety of chromosomal, phenotypical and hormonal shapes. The space between male and female is small indeed. Tanis reminds us that

> Day and night are not fixed entities with clear boundaries where one ends and the other begins; every day contains both dawn and dusk, which create a time in which day and night exist together in the same moment as one moves into the next. . . . God also created liminal spaces in which the elements of creation overlap and merge. (Tanis 2003, pp. 57–8)

It is these 'liminal spaces' that intersex and transgender people occupy as male turns into female and female turns into male. The idea of male and female being opposite ends of a mono-dimensional spectrum does not serve us well. Rather, gender identity is multi-faceted and multi-dimensional that changes over time and is dependent on the cultural reading of any one individual or community.

From the nineteenth century onwards, medical intervention in the lives and bodies of intersex people has sought to enforce the 'one-body-one-sex rule' (Dreger 1998, p. 197). Dreger argues that despite the many cultural changes of the twentieth century the 'one-body-one-sex rule' is alive and well. She states:

> [T]hat rule continues to be driven . . . by . . . an interest in keeping male/female gender distinctions and a concomitant interest in retaining a clear division between heterosexuality and homosexuality and in supporting . . . heterosexuality. (Dreger 1998, p. 197)

Kessler purports that intervention in the lives of intersex people is not because intersexuality threatens the person's life but rather their culture (Kessler 1990, cited in Dreger 1998, p. 197), or rather, I would add, it is the intersex person's ambiguity that threatens the existence of a dominant, patriarchal, heterosexual culture.

While it is difficult to estimate accurately the incidence of various intersex conditions, Fausto-Sterling estimates that up to 1 per cent of all births are intersexed (Fausto-Sterling 1992). It is medical intervention that has rendered intersex people invisible and their bodies as contested territory to be 'corrected' and 'normalized'.

Leslie Feinberg provides an excellent documentation of intersex and transgender people throughout many ancient societies in all parts of the world (Feinberg 1996). Intersex and transgender people in ancient civilizations inhabited spaces as wise ones, shamans, healers, and spiritual leaders. These spaces straddle the dualistic poles of male and female.

Feinberg argues that the rise of patriarchal societies in the ancient world heralded the end of social spaces delineated for intersex and differently gendered people. The ownership of property in a patriarchal society requires clarity between male and female – hence, laws that restrict the rights of intersex and transgender people, as they undermine a patriarchal system based on ownership and inheritance. Feinberg argues that this was rooted in the development of societies based on class distinctions and the ownership of property (Feinberg 1996, p. 51).

> Communal societies in which labour was voluntary and collective gave way to unequal societies in which those who owned wealth forced others to work for them – an enforced social relationship of masters and slaves . . . Everything that had once been considered natural was turned on its head in the service of the new owning classes. (Feinberg 1996, p. 52)

Feinberg states that it was law, including religious law, which codified the new social order (Feinberg 1996, p. 52). Interestingly, Feinberg suggests that it is class and the rise of patriarchy, rather than Judaism, that is at the root of the oppression of transgender people and women (Feinberg 1996, p. 53).

The prevalence of differently gendered bodies throughout all ages is, therefore, self-evident.

Jesus – gender queer, virgin born, intersex, transman

Mollenkott (Mollenkott 2001, p. 105) proposes that Jesus was chromosomally female. For this theory she relies upon an article by Kessel (Kessel 1983) where he states that female virgin birth is biologically possible, but that any offspring would have XX chromosomes, therefore being chromosomally female themselves. Kessel further suggests that Jesus' male appearance was due to a subsequent sex reversal, again biologically possible. Thus, Jesus was chromosomally female, but phenotypically male. Mollenkott ties this into the Genesis narrative of God who is both male and female and neither, and thereby a Jesus who is equally both and neither, encompassing the breadth of 'natural' human gender and sex diversity (Mollenkott 2001, p. 106). Further Mollenkott argues that following Kessel's approach it is intersex people or female-to-male trans-people who come closest to a physical resemblance to Jesus being chromosomally female and socially male (Mollenkott 2001, p. 106).

Whatever we might think of Kessel's theory, Jesus was certainly not confined to binary gender roles, and as Mollenkott suggests (Mollenkott 2001, p. 107), we must allow room for a Christ himself and Christ herself.

Moxnes (Moxnes 2003, pp. 72–90) suggests that Jesus occupied queer space by virtue of his social location and the location of his followers. Jesus' followers put themselves outside the norms of society by leaving their homes and their social gender roles to follow Jesus. By leaving their place in the household, Moxnes suggests they rendered themselves liable to the accusation of being eunuchs – their very gender identity was put into question for upsetting the gender norms of their time. Leaving this socially privileged position was to abdicate something of their maleness and masculinity. It was the dominant social order of the patriarchal household that Jesus sought to challenge from the marginal place of outsider.

Moxnes presents a critique of interpretations of Matthew 19.12 and suggests that, throughout the centuries and even today, these verses cause some problems. This, he suggests, is due to interpreters' presuppositions about masculinity, both of Jesus and his followers.

> The eunuch is a highly problematic and ambiguous figure who, because he is a male figure, threatens the very idea of masculinity. To imagine Jesus or his disciples as eunuchs, as men who were physically unfit for marriage, unable to perform sexually, is perhaps an unsettling picture. But this strange and uncomfortable picture of the eunuch is a useful place to start. (Moxnes 2003, p. 74)

The image of the eunuch is one of an 'outsider', someone who is rejected by society, ritually unclean and excluded from the mainstream social discourse. Jesus takes on the role of 'outsider', thereby challenging our very image of what masculinity is and the form that God would choose to appear to men (and women and everybody else).

Matthew 19.12 has often been interpreted in the context of the previous verses where Jesus is discussing marriage and divorce with the Pharisees. The most common understanding of these verses, then, is that they suggest celibacy and a chaste life are callings that some people have. However, Moxnes suggests that Matthew 19.12 may have been an independent saying of Jesus (Moxnes 2003, p. 75). Moxnes suggests that the term 'eunuch' was used to slander Jesus and his disciples, and Jesus used this in his response. The first two types of eunuchs would have been well known, those from birth and those who had been castrated, that is, by human intervention. Moxnes suggests that in the third category Jesus was referring to his disciples, as they had chosen to follow him, rather than marry, thus 'for the sake of the kingdom'. Moxnes suggests:

> [T]he term 'eunuch' was commonly used . . . of someone who was physically (made) *unfit* for marriage and incapable of performing sexually. The central question is therefore whether the last group was parallel to the others in this respect, or whether 'eunuch' was here used in another, figurative meaning. (Moxnes 2003, p. 75)

Moxnes suggests that Matthew 19.12 could be compared to other sayings of Jesus where he discusses other social marginalized groups, such as tax collectors, for example, in Matthew 21.31 and Luke 15.1–2. Moxnes argues that, since Jesus did not simply refute the saying, it was indeed used as a slander of Jesus and his followers, casting doubt on their masculinity and social location (Moxnes 2003, p. 89). Rather than question the saying Jesus identifies himself with the term 'eunuch'. The possibility that Jesus may have been, either literally or figuratively, a eunuch is one rejected by ancient and modern interpreters, since the masculinity of Jesus is sacrosanct. Jesus is constructed as the most masculine, most 'real' man; his divinity has been inextricably linked with his masculinity.

Moxnes suggests that in using the term eunuch Jesus placed himself 'permanently out of place, in a liminal position' (Moxnes 2003, p. 89). He further suggests that the term 'queer' is the only modern equivalent which captures this essence of being beyond categorization, a term which goes beyond gender or sexuality and encompasses 'power, social roles, place in hierarchies . . . all aspects of identity' (Moxnes 2003, p. 90).

Jesus' queer identity is not simply to be read in terms of sexuality, but he is truly gender queer. Jesus is our own *transcestor*: 'the challenge of eunuchs was that they could not be securely placed, they were in a position of "betwixt and between", in a permanent liminal position' (Moxnes 2003, p. 80).

In entering queer space, we find normative boundaries blurred, dualistic definitions refuted and the creation of permissive identities. It is in this space that we enter 'the kingdom of heaven', a world without the confines of traditional, patriarchal structures, systems and roles. Jesus' notion of the reign of God 'questions identities and blurs distinctions' of the normative social categories and social roles of the time (Bohache 2006, p. 509).

Jesus' cryptic response to the disciples' questions about whether it is better to abstain from marriage leads to the discussion of the categories of eunuchs. This response was to challenge prevailing social norms and gender roles. This would turn the patriarchal male household structure on its head. Bohache speculates about Jesus' response:

> Could Jesus not be referring to a broad category of people who, from their birth, have not 'fitted' the predominant expectations of gender and sexuality? In effect, Jesus in this saying about eunuchs has not only entered queer space, but has 'queered' the discussion of marriage. (Bohache 2006, p. 510)

Bohache refers to the work of Theodore Jennings who suggests:

> The saying of Jesus is scandalous . . . Like many of Jesus' sayings, this one is shocking in daring to link the reign of God with apparently absurd or outrageous behaviour . . . associate[ing] followers of Jesus who have renounced family structures with stigmatized or marginalized groups in the Hellenistic world. (Jennings 2003, p. 153)

Bohache argues that if, as Moxnes suggests, the term 'eunuch' was used as a slur against Jesus and his disciples then we have hit upon

> an essential concept for a queer understanding of Jesus: today there are many for whom the word 'queer' is a volatile word, since it originated as a slur among our opponents, but activists and others have reclaimed the word and used it proudly. (Bohache 2006, p. 510)

Freyne suggests that a hallmark of Jesus' Judaism was a concentration on God's compassion and a radically inclusive Israel as envisaged in Isaiah. Freyne argues that it was this vision that leads Jesus to travel to Jerusalem and his death. Jesus' saying about the eunuchs recalls the prophesy in Isaiah 56 of an inclusive community (Freyne 2004).

Thus, it is clear, that these verses in Matthew 19 are an example of Jesus' message of inclusivity to those on the margins of society.

Eunuchs One and All

The promise of 'a house of prayer for all people' in Isaiah 56 is not simply a promise that eunuchs would be allowed. Rather it is an unrestrained revolution to the existing order of who can approach God. Ritually unclean, living at the margins of society and unable to produce offspring that would continue the family line to provide security in old age, the eunuch was reviled.

Koch suggests that the last 11 chapters of Isaiah commencing at chapter 56 present many instances of gender dissent and social queerness (Koch 2006, p. 381). He suggests that

> This eschatological vision [of Isaiah 56–67] represents a freedom that is exhilarating, and a reframing of righteousness that is within the purview of all – without respect to physicality, nationality, or sexuality. . . . An eschatological hope for social organization that is free from the constrictions of gender roles. (Koch 2006, p. 383).

The Matthean eunuch verses are a mirror to the Isaiah 56 passage which extends the kingdom of God to eunuchs with a special place greater than that of sons and daughters. So then, the genealogy of Christ, which Matthew commences with, is radicalized to include even those who cannot procreate, even those whose bloodline has been lost to society, even those whom society considers most marginal and outside the boundaries of normative behaviour. These verses encapsulate the radical inclusivity of Jesus' message – there is no one who is marginal in God's eyes, all are included (Koch 2006).

This vision of the realm of God is one that celebrates our God-given gender identity and how we choose to express it.

Reclaiming Identities

It is easy to assume that all societies have placed those who are differently gendered at the margins; however, Ringrose's provocative history of eunuchs in Byzantium from the sixth to twelfth centuries challenges this notion. She presents a compelling history of the social construction of eunuchs, whose gender was other than male or female, who occupied a liminal, marginal space, yet were socially powerful (Ringrose 2003).

Eunuchs in Byzantium occupied a distinct social gender category, a third gender, incorporated into the culture of the day, occupying positions of social power and trust. Ringrose cites numerous examples of youths and adult men castrated in order to advance their careers in the Church or politics or to protect the dynastic line of succession, that is, to exclude them from fathering children. Interestingly, she also refers to the story of a seven-year old girl who entered a monastery, who was assumed to be a eunuch (Ringrose 2003, p. 62).

This whisper of the presence of differently gendered female-bodied individuals is a clue to the presence of female-to-male individuals, who are often hard to find, if not invisible. Ringrose suggests there are:

> Many stories of women who pretended to be eunuchs in order to enjoy some of the freedom of choice reserved for men. In doing so, they capitalized on society's assumption they were eunuchs rather than women when they took on roles attributed to men or eunuchs. (Ringrose 2003, p. 65)

These passing women are our transgender ancestors. My gut tells me some of these were more than likely transmen, binding their breasts and living as male a life as they could. Eunuchs held a 'transcendent ambiguity' (Ringrose 2003, p. 65) which enabled them to move through social categories and the dominant norms of behaviour. Further, this ambiguity was counter to the order of the Graeco-Roman world: although Byzantium made a social place for eunuchs, other societies were not so accommodating.

> Byzantine culture and society constructed a collective identity for its eunuchs . . . perhaps the ultimate case of socially constructed gender [where] the primary indicators of gender were not sexual object hoice but rather physical appearance, societal function, relationship to reproduction, and capacity for relating to what we would consider the spiritual world. Eunuchs represented a very special 'other'. (Ringrose 2003, p. 83)

Eunuchs then were fascinating, spiritual, powerful 'beings' who were able to move through the social order of the day. By the tenth century, Ringrose suggests that eunuchs in the Church had begun to assume a more positive role than the court eunuch (Ringrose 2003, p. 86).

Rereading and queering biblical texts is not something that started with modern queer theologians. Indeed, Theophylaktos of Ohrid, in the eleventh century, was asking questions about Daniel. The Byzantines read the prophet Daniel as a court eunuch, and in their social context this makes most sense for his role (Ringrose 2003). Equally, we now know that the Hebrew words used for court official are the same as those for eunuch. The Byzantines were on the right track. The story of Daniel follows all the classical markers for a Byzantine eunuch: he was reared in the king's household and selected to become a courtier; he was attractive and eternally youthful; he acted as an intermediary; he functioned as a guardian of sacred space; he interpreted dreams and visions. Most importantly, he was the trusted servant of the king (Ringrose 2003, p. 89).

West suggests that: 'If queer theory is about the politics of resistance and the indeterminacy of identity (and it is) then Daniel is one of the queerest books of the Bible' (West 2006a, p. 427).

Daniel's fluid identity resists categorization and 'reawakens the ancient silences of queer spiritual ancestry' (West 2006a, p. 429). Daniel's gender identity as a eunuch enabled him to mediate not only the gendered world but also the spiritual and physical worlds. There are numerous examples of gender-variant people acting as 'mediators of the sacred' (West 2006a, p. 430). Similarly, in the book of Esther eunuchs function as 'a third term' or a 'third mode of articulation', able to cross boundaries between male and female space and, as West suggests, are the only ones who hold all the information and ultimately are the ones with real power in this narrative (West 2006b, p. 285).

Huerta identifies *agule* (like men) and *okule* (like women) from the East African Lugbara people, who are spiritual intermediaries or mediums; the Russian *enarees* (unmanly ones) who are third-gender priests; and the Native American *berdache* (two-spirited ones) as our queer spiritual ancestors (Huerta 1999, cited in West 2006a, p. 430). We who are boundary crossers can use this gift to enter into spiritual space and create pathways for change (Wilson 1995; West 2006a).

Ringrose suggests that in Byzantine culture sharp distinctions between earthly and spiritual realms were not drawn; instead, there was a 'spectrum of overlapping domains' (Ringrose 2003, pp. 142–62). Eunuchs were believed to be able to transcend these domains because of their social and physical ambiguity. Parallels of, and indeed confusion between, eunuchs and angels were made. Eunuchs occupied a distinct spiritual territory closed to others.

> [B]oth angels and eunuchs shared a strong quality of 'otherness' . . . Both also shared a kind of third-gender quality that allowed them to transcend the differences between the worlds of earthly materialism and heavenly spirituality. (Ringrose 2003, pp. 161–2)

The social location of those who do not fit within traditional notions of gender, whether due to sexuality or gender identity, has challenged the norms of many societies. Whether it is in ancient biblical societies, first-century Palestine, the Byzantine Empire, or in twenty-first century Western society, differently gendered people find a way to create liminal space that is both in and between the categories of male and female, masculine and feminine. Our recent history has catalogued the re-emergence of a visible gender different population, of an intersex human rights movement, and of the queering of dominant notions of what it is to be a man or a woman. Spaces that are both and neither are hard-won territory, often contested and held with an expectation of being overrun.

The emergence of the modern transgender civil rights movement in the last 40 years (at the time of writing) has enabled us to find one another and find places to call our own, to create identities that do not follow common narrative paths, to call for our acceptance as full members of society. We must remember, however, that we have always been here, and that our history begins at the very beginning of human history.

Made in the image of God

The idea of God as male and female, both and neither, is not new. Many images are used throughout Scripture to characterize the nature of God. Newell and Gunn suggest that perhaps even God is not clear about God's own gender identity when God describes godself as both 'we' and 'I'.

> [With] the creation of humankind, that is, the creature in the image of God (Gen. 1:26–30) we see movement against that desire to differentiate. Blurring the binary poles . . . Yet in all this careful defining separating and opposing there is a curious slippage. God 'himself' is unsure whether he is plural or singular . . . While humankind is one (him/it) it is also plural – male and female (them). (Newell and Gunn 1993, p. 23)

The fluidity of God's gender identity is represented in human beings: we are created in the very likeness of God (Gen. 1.26). The 'earth creature', *ādām*, was not a gendered being, but rather, full of all the gender diversity possible in God, full of all maleness and femaleness, and every other gender possibility besides. It is only when the second human creature is created, out of *ādām*, that human beings are differentiated into male and female (Tanis 2003, p. 58). This 'virgin' birth is a foretaste of the virgin birth that is to come in Jesus.

Tanis (2003, p. 61) argues that in our reading of the second account of the creation story, in Genesis 2, we must realize that the 'earth-creature', *ādām,* became *man* and *woman* after *ādām*'s deep sleep. Two new distinct gendered beings were created, where previously only one, multi-gendered being existed. *Ādām* was not left unchanged by this process. It is suggested then, that 'If completeness comes from having both male and female, then a person who possessed both is a return to the original completion in the earth creature' (Tanis 2003, p. 61).

In Carden's discussion of the creation story, he suggests Jewish tradition would understand that a two-gender-only system is not presented in these accounts of creation. Rather, that the first human being was an androgynous being, and that

> Jewish Kabbalah understands that Genesis 1 is a textual representation of the Kabbalistic Tree of Life . . . The Tree consists of male, female and intermediate . . . while being androgynous, the Tree of Life also embraces sexuality [and] provides a space for a more polymorphous and egalitarian sexuality. The Kabbalistic Tree suggests that the androgyne is the model for each and every human, that male and female represent a fluid continuum in each individual that must be brought into harmony. (Carden 2006, p. 98)

Citing Gross, Carden (2006) points out that Rabbinic Judaism had a clear understanding that not everyone was born male or female. He states that Rabbinic Judaism used the words *tumtum* to denote a person whose physical sex could not be determined by their genitalia and *'aylonith* to describe a woman without a womb (Gross 1999, p. 78).

We, who are gender queer, transgender, or intersex, are indeed made in the image of God. Our search for identity and an understanding of our bodies, and the narratives they tell, recalls the complex nature of God. Our gender contradictions and our complicated stories simply reflect who we have been, are, and will become. God's very self contains all facets of gender, all dimensions, expressions, and characteristics held together in one divine being, one divine being who is not one but three. Gender and gender identity is at the heart of the mystery which is God. When an intersex or gender-different child is born, this is a moment to celebrate the act of creation, the act when God differentiated human beings into different kinds.

At the least, we are called to embrace all that is female within us, as well as all that is male, as well as all that fits neither category. If those who experience their physical, biological, hormonal and chromosomal selves in congruence can embrace a more fluid gender identity that holds lightly to that which is masculine or feminine, then we who are at odds with our biology will find the liberation to choose a path towards integration. A model of gender, which calls us to a place where gender is not polarized into the oppositional male and female seems entirely consistent with the liberation that we find in Christ and a return to a place of original blessing (Fox 1983).

Trans-sexualities

Transgender and intersex bodies, once constructed as non-reproductive and sexual, are being reclaimed as the sites of sexual and erotic freedom. Intersex and transgender people are sexual beings, with sexual bodies. We are reclaiming our identities and the right to inhabit these bodies, these bodies which are contradictory, confounding and often beyond description. Our male/female/other genitals are unique places where male and female come together, recalling that time of creation when each one of us, the world over, was neither male nor female. These bodies hold the secret of intense sexual pleasure, of difference, and confront our ideas about being gay, lesbian, straight or bisexual. These are bodies, simply bodies, which can experience the god-given joys of sexual pleasure.

You might find these bodies anywhere, in your local bar, in a sex club in San Francisco, in the pages of a personal ad, or sitting next to you in the pew. These bodies will challenge your ideas about physical pleasure and perhaps about your own identity.

It is for these bodies that we must find a place of honour and move from a phallocentric-deficit model, where transgender people are defined by the presence or absence of a penis. It is not a penis which makes a man, nor its absence which makes a woman; rather it is some innate, yet intangible quality, some knowing, some Spirit, that leads us to conclude our gender identity. Many of us have sacrificed bodily pleasure at the hands of the surgeons' knife in the pursuit of normative genitalia.

Developing a Transgender Inclusive Theology

What then of transgender theology? What might this be? Perhaps, a theology beyond dualistic gender paradigms, which seeks to reveal the existence of transgender, intersex and gender-queer people in the narrative of God's relationship with humankind. There is considerable theology which seeks to be inclusive, yet fails in this task, for simply replacing 'he' with 'she' and 'mother' for 'father' does not create the radical project that Jesus had in mind in his sayings about eunuchs. No, we need to go much further than this. Our notions about the binary constructions of gender, and society itself, are being called into question. Notions about maleness, femaleness and otherness must be explored. We are not just the sons and daughters of the creator; we are the children; we are not just brothers and sisters, but we are siblings. We are individuals within, outwith and beyond gender, we are difficult to categorize, for we are inhabiting the liminal spaces, the spaces 'betwixt and between'. This is the ground upon which we fashion ourselves and our lives. It is this ground which we are called to inhabit, this contested territory, for this is God's territory.

References

Althaus-Reid, Marcella (2003), *The Queer God* (London: Routledge).

Bohache, Thomas (2006), 'Matthew', in Deryn Guest, Robert E. Goss, Mona West and Thomas Bohache, eds, *The Queer Bible Commentary* (London: SCM Press), pp. 487–516.

Carden, Michael (2006), 'Genesis/Bereshit', in Deryn Guest, Robert E. Goss,

Mona West and Thomas Bohache, eds, *The Queer Bible Commentary* (London: SCM Press), pp. 21–60.

Dreger, Alice Domurat (1998), *Hermaphrodites and the Medical Invention of Sex* (Cambridge: Harvard University Press).

Fausto-Sterling, Anne (1992), *Myths of Gender: Biological Theories About Women and Men* (New York: Basic Books).

Feinberg, Leslie (1996), *Transgender Warriors* (Boston: Beacon Press).

Foucault, Michel (1980), *Power/Knowledge* (New York: Pantheon Books).

Fox, Matthew (1983), *Original Blessing* (Santa Fe: Bear).

Freyne, Sean (2004), *Jesus a Jewish Galilean: A New Reading of the Jesus-Story* (London: T &T Clark).

Goss, Robert E. (1993), *Jesus Acted Up: A Gay and Lesbian Manifesto* (New York: Harper Collins).

Gross, Sally (1999), 'Intersexuality and Scripture', *Theology and Sexuality* 11, pp. 65–74.

Guest, Deryn, Robert E. Goss, Mona West and Thomas Bohache, eds (2006), *The Queer Bible Commentary* (London: SCM Press).

de la Huerta, Christian (1999), *Coming Out Spiritually: The Next Step* (New York: Jeremy P. Tarcher/Putnam).

Jennings, Theodore (2003), *The Man Jesus Loved* (Cleveland, OH: Pilgrim Press).

Kessel, Edward I. (1983), 'A Proposed Biological Interpretation of the Virgin Birth', *Journal of the American Scientific Affliation* 35, pp. 129–36.

Kessler, Suzanne J. (1990), 'The Medical Construction of Gender: Case Management of Intersexed Infants', *Signs* 16:1, pp. 3–26.

Koch, Timothy (2006), 'Isaiah', in Deryn Guest, Robert E. Goss, Mona West and Thomas Bohache, eds (2006), *The Queer Bible Commentary* (London: SCM Press), pp. 371–85.

Mollenkott, Virginia Ramey (2001), *Omnigender* (Cleveland, OH: The Pilgrim Press).

Moxnes, Halvor (2003), *Putting Jesus in His Place A Radical Vision of Household and Kingdom* (Louisville: Westminster John Knox Press).

Newell, Danna N. and David M. Gunn (1993), *Gender, Promise and Power: The Subject of the Bible's First Story* (Nashville: Abingdon Press).

Ringrose, Kathryn M. (2003), *The Perfect Servant: Eunuchs and the Social Construction of Gender in Byzantium* (Chicago: University of Chicago Press).

Strong, James (2001), *Dictionary of Bible Words* (Nashville: Thomas Nelson Publishers).

Tanis, Justin (2003), *Transgendered: Theology, Ministry and Communities of Faith* (Cleveland, OH: Pilgrim Press).

West, Mona (2006a), 'Daniel', in Deryn Guest, Robert E. Goss, Mona West and Thomas Bohache, eds (2006), *The Queer Bible Commentary* (London: SCM Press), pp. 427–31.

West, Mona (2006b), 'Esther', in Deryn Guest, Robert E. Goss, Mona West and Thomas Bohache, eds (2006), *The Queer Bible Commentary* (London: SCM Press), pp. 278–85.

Wilson, Nancy (1995), *Our Tribe: Queer Folks, God, Jesus and the Bible* (New York: Harper).

11

God's New Frock

JOHN CLIFFORD

I first performed this play in the Changing House at the Tron Theatre, Glasgow, on 5 and 6 April 2002. The production was made possible through the generosity and support of Tron management and staff. This revised version of the script was performed at the Tron Theatre, 12–15 March 2003, and then at the Traverse Theatre, Edinburgh, 16–19 April 2003.

Performer	John Clifford
Composer/Musician	Robert Burlin
Director	Lorenzo Mele
Producer	Steven Gale
Costume Designer	Morna Baxter
Spotlight Operator	Kirstie Neville

Hello

Hello ladies, hello gentlemen. Hello men, hello women,

Hello those of you who are not ladies and are not gentlemen,

And not men and not women

but like me

maybe something in between or maybe something that's a bit of both or something

or somebody

that has never been thought of or imagined yet.

Somebody or something this evening may even bring into being.

Welcome.

Welcome to this precious time, this precious hour we're going to spend together.

This hour that has never happened quite like this before

and will never happen quite like this again.

I thought of doing something very simple and perhaps something a little corny

I thought I'd tell you a story.

An important story.

An important story because we're all important people, we all of us matter, though the world puts a lot of effort into telling us the opposite.

An important story because I've been told it explains who we are and how we came into this world.

So it must be about the most important story there is.

I expect you've heard it before.

And maybe like me when you were first told it you were very little.

And you were told it was the story of God.

Who was very big.

And what he did when he made the world.

And that means it's also a story about me. About me and about you when we were all boys or maybe girls

or maybe something in between, or maybe a bit of both or maybe something

or somebody

that has never been thought of or imagined yet.

And you may think that fanciful,

but let me tell you,

ladies or gentlemen or maybe something in between,

that part of us is divine and does live up high in the sky, or maybe deep down below in the pits of hell, or maybe in both places at once

and that part of us just like the god of the story does create the world every day

every day we get out of bed

every day we get out of bed and open our eyes

we create the world

we create the world we're going to inhabit for the whole of the day to come

and we do it again and again.

And it could be any day we want.

Only because we're maybe a little old or a little tired and certainly have absolutely no confidence in ourselves every single day it's usually just the bloody same

it's the office or the school or the hospital or whatever and then the telly

every day the same

except for tonight, tonight is different.

And so today ladies and gentlemen and everyone outrageous in between

today at this moment that has never happened before quite like this

and will never ever happen quite like this again

today I am going to tell you about the beginning.

The beginning of everything.

This story. An old story.

This very old story.

That I heard

when I was still a boy, or maybe a girl, or maybe something in between.

And I believed every word.

And then a day came when I forgot this story

forgot I'd ever heard it

forgot I'd ever lived it

forgot I'd ever believed it

and tried to believe in evolution instead

or the big bang or something

and I thought the old story had just withered away.

And then I came to understand what the trouble is.

The trouble is that it didn't. Wither away. This story.

It's still there deep deep in the heart of us.

The story is in us and we are in the story.

We are its heroines, or maybe its heroes, or maybe something in between,

And we live through it, and it will live through us.

And until we somehow discover a new story to understand ourselves

We'll never escape it.

We will go on and on living inside it for ever and ever.

So. I hope you're sitting comfortably.

And then I'll begin.

Now once upon a time

a long long time ago

in a far far distant country . . .

and it really was a long long time ago, it really really was.

Because it was all so amazingly long ago it all happened before time had even been invented.

Before time ever was:

or anything else for that matter.

It was a time and it was a space where there was nothing at all.

Absolutely nothing at all except for this one being, apparently,

this one being who thought he was very big

but who actually,

in the middle of this great big nothing,

was really very very small.

And this being, who liked to think of himself as very big, this very big being has many different names, and very important names too.

I mean they must have been important, because for thousands of years we have been killing each other over them.

Killing each other over which is the right name to use.

We burn each other to death and imprison each other and torture each other with red hot pincers or electric shocks.

And you may think all that happened a long long time ago,

but let me tell you, ladies, gentlemen, and everyone in between, that in a country not so very far away there is one group of people who systematically oppress and insult another group of people because they use different names for this being. One group call him Jehovah and the other group call him Allah.

And in a city that's even closer, there are people who line a street on the way to a primary school, brave, upright, manly people who line the street and yell SCUM! and FILTH! at four-year-old children because even though they use the same name for this being, 'God', they seem to understand it differently.

So you see we're entering really dangerous territory here. And we've hardly begun.

I'm not sure I know what to do for the best.

But I'll tell you what I'll do:

Just for the moment, and to get the story going, what I'll do is call this being God.

And then we'll see.

Cause that's what he likes, this being, and although he says he's all powerful he's actually very easily hurt.

So we'll call him God for now, and keep him happy.

But I want you to do something for me: I want you to promise me that

deep in the secretest corner, the secretest corner of your innermost hearts,

you'll keep for yourselves the right to call this Being anything you want.

And you do really have the right to do this because you are the heroes of this story, or maybe its heroines, or maybe something in between, and so you really can call this being anything you secretly choose.

You might want to call him Terry. Or possibly Jim. Or Malcolm or Edith or Elizabeth or Jane.

Only that might get us into even worse trouble because he tended to ferociously insist on the fact that he was male.

Very ferociously. Very very very ferociously, and also

and this is very important because you'll get in the most terrible trouble if you ignore this one,

he used to insist he was all alone in the world and there was no one like him.

Anywhere.

And that's kind of sad, when you think about it, because he must have been so lonely.

And besides there are Gods everywhere if you think about it. Under that chair. In the eaves of the roof. In the lighting box. And in the secretest corner of your own deep hearts. Which is another reason why you can call this being, this him, or this her, or this something in between, absolutely anything you like.

But he wouldn't have that. He'd rather be lonely he said, and he used to threaten the most terrible torments on anyone who dared to suggest otherwise. And not just on them, who said it, or who even thought it, but on their children too.

And even on the children of their children.

He's like a drunk in a bar that'll pick a fight with anyone who seems to dare to hint that's he not a real man . . .

And like any drunk in any bar the chances are he's talking absolute shite.

But you still have to be careful.

So where were we?

We were a long long way away

A long long long time ago

So long it was before the beginning of time

When there was this being

all on his own, apparently,

and apparently most emphatically male,

floating on the waters

And oh dear me

When I think waters, when I think waters . . .

I think womb.

And I get the strangest feeling, ladies and gentlemen, heroes and heroines and maybe also something in between,

I get the strangest feeling that that's where he is.

In the womb.

And that means when he says all that bit about being all alone and all male and all that

that means he's lying.

And me a little wolf cub too.

Because that's what I was, ladies, gentlemen and something in betweens,

that's what I was when I first heard this story,

a wolf cub. All young and trusting with my little woggle.

Hearing about God being all male and all powerful and all alone

floating on the waters.

And he'd been in the womb all along.

Just like me.

But let's not be like him, let's not get all vindictive, let's be calm and reasonable and just try to see it through his eyes

and imagine what it felt like

what it felt like floating in the womb.

Not imagine so much as try to remember
because we've all been there
even if we've forgotten how it was.
But even if we can't remember, part of us is still there
and even if it feels impossible to go back there
we can at least begin to try.
So what we have to do, heroes and heroines and possibly either or both,
what we have to do is this:
close our eyes
close our eyes very tight and shut out the noise of the world
– and we absolutely have to try this –
close our eyes and remember
floating on the water
floating in the water
and the warm water all around
no light no dark
no up and no down
no before no after
no left and no right
no right no wrong
and absolutely no need to do anything at all.
Bliss. Pure bliss.
And if this was a sensible story
this would be the end of it.

Only it would have no beginning and it would have no end.

Only this.

This bliss.

But then this is not a sensible story.

This is our story.

This is about us. This is about us being born.

And about God being born too.

None of this ever turns up in the story.

Because he'd forgotten it. God. Forgotten all about it. Couldn't bear to remember it.

None of us can. Remember being born. Too painful.

But if you watch a baby God being born,

if you watch a baby –

and I won't call them human because we're not, really, when we first came into the world,

it's only later that humanness settles upon us and shuts us in.

But when we're born, these beings,

us, these amazing beings,

born into chaos and confusion

into the bright naked lights into the naked place where we have to gulp for air

we try to make sense of it.

We divide light from dark, day from night.

We create the world. Create the world every day of our lives.

And there I am, look I've just been born

A doctor with a white mask is holding me upside down

And I'm crying fit to burst

But still part of me is creating

Dividing light from dark

Light from dark, upper from lower, water from dry land, good from evil, masculine from feminine, *ying* from *yang*, on from off, one from zero.

And this produces day and night and the ocean and the continents and the animals and the fish and bricks and mortar, concrete and clay, aluminium and steel

and those fighter planes that circle above our heads

and we go on.

We go on and on, making big creatures and little creatures, creatures that moved on land and creatures that moved on the sea and creatures that flew in the air, on and on, elephants and goats and humming birds. On and on. Leopards and fig trees and mushrooms and diamonds and strange little creatures whose names have been forgotten, or not even thought up yet, on and on,

Buffaloes and butterflies and the possibility of orange marmalade, on and on.

And then we stop and look around.

Because it is so beautiful.

And we look at it all and say.

Yes, it is good. It is very good.

And then God had a rest, and invented Sunday.

And apparently he invented church services too.

And look there's me when I heard this, still just a boy, sitting in a church pew and wriggling,

all scratchy in my wolf cub uniform

and I believed every word of it, as you do at moments like these,

when you're very young and grown-ups tell you things, even grown-ups in a church wearing odd white frocks, 'only it's not a frock William you naughty boy, men don't wear frocks. It's a vestment. And that's different.'

And I didn't understand that really and felt a bit silly because that's something else, something else that people tell you:

And if you don't understand what they're telling you it must be your fault.

So I never said I never understood

Just as I never said I never liked being called William

Because they'd never understand that

Or that when I looked in the mirror and saw a boy

I had the strangest feeling that someone had made the most terrible mistake.

Just as I knew they had in the Bible, because it says

God created human beings twice over.

Once before he went to sleep and invented Sunday and then again afterwards.

And the first time he told us we could have dominion over the fish of the sea and the fowl of the air and every living thing that moveth over the earth,

and we like that bit, because it means we can eat pork sausages and cut down the rain forest and feed dead cow to other cows and still feel self-righteous

and he also told us he made us in his own image, which may be a bit puzzling if you happen to have breasts and a womb but which is still on the whole quite flattering so we remember those bits.

But what we forget is the bit where he says

Male and female created he them.

Or possibly him. Or possibly singular of dual gender, the authorities differ, and an obscure rabbinical school has speculated on the androgynous nature of the first human being.

And what that implies is the androgynous nature of God, too, which is highly embarrassing for everybody, and so has also been forgotten.

But we will remember.

We will remember in spite of the version of the story everybody knows. Adam and God and the finger, it could be you, and God creating man.

And when we say man, we mean man. I must apologize to those of you who identify yourselves as heroines, but at this point in time, apparently, you do not exist.

There are no females in the world anywhere. Apparently.

The universe is a kind of gigantic old-fashioned golf club from which women are definitely barred.

See the story goes that he made men from dust. And he made women from a bone. But only as an afterthought. And for a certain type of mentality, that is the story's main attraction.

Because this one is so much more convenient. For priests and patriarchs and golfers.

They like the fact he made men from dust and from earth and from mud and I suppose at least a little spit. Or maybe a lot of spit, I don't know, I've never tried it. Like you'd make a cup. Or a saucer. Or a plate. Only more complicated, because of the insides and all.

And when he had finished making you men, inside as well as out, he breathed on you, and you became alive. And that's why the word for wind, *ruach* in semitic languages is the same for breath and the same for soul, and I like that.

And because at that time he was still proud and happy and he made you the most beautiful garden that could ever be imagined. And he planted it. He was his own seed catalogue, and he planted it with his hand.

And there were beautiful trees that gave sweet fruit, and beautiful flowers that gave sweet scent, and hot and cold running water, and gorgeous butterflies, and the most delightful singing birds.

And that's where you lived, you and Adam, you the heroes of this story, you lived in this beautiful garden. And were utterly miserable.

And God saw this, because he wasn't altogether daft, and God said:

'It is not good for Man to live alone.'

And he was right, of course, it's not good for anyone to live alone, not alone alone. Not alone without anyone even to see at the supermarket, and so of course you were miserable. Poor thing.

Anyway, there he was, man should not live alone, sounding magisterial, but actually making it all up as he went along. Because he gathered together all the hundreds and hundreds of creatures he had made and paraded them in front of Adam. And he had to give them all names, must have been exhausting, and also have a good look at them and see if anyone of them would make a suitable companion.

And the thing is, and I'm really sorry to tell you this, you who identify yourselves as women and so are the heroines of this story, that you were obviously an afterthought, because it was only after Adam had looked at all the animals, and turned them all down: turned down the pet dog and the pet cat and the pet gerbil, the pet tiger and the pet warthog and the pet bunny rabbit, the pet donkey and the pet elephant and the pet dung beetle, only after he had turned down all these beautiful creatures as his companions that God invented anaesthetic, whether gas, or injection, or just a single look from his terrible eye, and Adam was fast asleep.

And when he woke up there was a woman beside him.

And also a strange hollow space just underneath his heart.

Now the first woman was Lilith, though we've been told she was Eve. But Lilith, apparently, took one look at Adam, and said: 'I don't want to live with him.' And ran off to the desert. God sent three angels after her to try to force her to return, but she was stronger than all of them, and never came back.

And so she was consigned to hatred and oblivion.

But I remember her. I remember her well. And were I the woman I once so desperately wanted to be, I think I might tell her story.

But I am not that woman, and never will be.

I am who I am, like the bush that is always burning.

And isn't it strange the way this story says that woman came from man, and how often have we believed it. And the whole world's organized as if it were true. As if men were the centre of things and women really only were an afterthought.

But when you think about it for a moment, it's so perfectly obvious that men come out of woman.

And so what's the moral of this. What's the moral of this holy wise and sacred story.

That if you're going to tell a lie make it a big one. Make it a whopper.

And the bigger the lie, the more people will want to believe it.

And they'll never change their minds, cause to change their minds they'll have to accept what idiots they all were in the first place.

You see, there's me, as a boy, listening to it. Listening to the man who's wearing a white frock that isn't a frock telling me all about it.

And I'm sitting in a pew in my wolf cub uniform, in my scratchy shorts and my neckerchief, and I'm not happy at all. Because I hate my woggle, I don't want to be with Akela and dib dib dib and do my best and climb trees and be brave and learn to tie knots.

I want to have a nice brown frock and be with brown owl and the brownies and learn how to be nice and bake cakes.

And that puzzles me.

I mean, there's men and there's women but who am I?

I don't seem to figure anywhere in this story, it's like God didn't create me at all, yet here I am, and I'm feeling utterly alone.

And we know it's not good to be alone.

And if only I'd known it, there was almost certainly another little wolf cub in the same room, somewhere, feeling just like I did, just as I know there'll be at least one here in this room, somewhere. There always is one. We get everywhere. We just have to hide, that's all.

Because we are just so dangerous.

And again if I'd known there was almost certainly in another room somewhere in the same town at least one girl who hated her silly frock and would have gladly swapped it for my scratchy shorts and run off to climb trees and be happy.

And if we could have . . . And if only we'd known . . .

Where was I?

In the garden. Adam and Eve were in the beautiful garden.

And they were happy, as we all were happy, once. Eating and sleeping and looking around. Looking around at the beautiful world.

At our beautiful world.

Being. Just being in the beautiful world.

And the deal was they could go anywhere they liked, and eat anything they liked, and have any number of hot baths, and any number of cold baths, and listen to any number of beautiful singing birds, and just be happy, be happy for ever and ever just so long as they didn't eat the fruit of one particular tree, the tree of the knowledge of good and evil.

That one over there.

That one over there with the gorgeous red fruit. The red fruit hanging from its branches.

The red fruit ripe and ready to eat.

And you don't need a degree in psychology to tell what happens next, nor the wisdom of hindsight either, it was all so obvious to everybody, except the people involved in it, and except to God too, apparently. And this is another of those moments when it's impossible to believe in the supposed all wisdom of God. In his all-seeing knowledge of the mysteries of his creation. The man was obviously a fool. A demiurge. A bungler.

And there's no need to invent the story of the serpent and the temptation of Eve to explain. It's just a cover-up that is, a diversionary tactic, to draw everyone's attention away from the real culprit: the incompetence of God himself.

But where was I?

They're eating, look they're eating the fruit for the very first time, and it tastes delicious, and they're looking at each other. Looking at each other as if for the very first time.

And then she sees he's got a prick.

And he sees she's got a cunt.

And for some reason that makes them both intensely ashamed.

And that was how he knew. That was how he knew what they had done.

He was walking in the garden, the story goes, walking in the garden in the cool of the day. And he was happy, perhaps. And they heard his voice. Perhaps he was singing.

This is the last time he walks the earth.

From now on he absents himself: he thunders from mountains, he sends down angels. He inspires prophets and sends down his own son.

He is a raging wind, he is a dove, a light in the heaven, a burning bush. And sometimes he is a still small voice.

But this is him, this is himself, walking down simply on the earth among us.

Walking down simply among us for the very last time.

And we hid from him. We were terribly terribly ashamed.

And that's how he knew.

And he was utterly furiously uncontrollably angry.

He told the woman: you will always be frightened of snakes, and that in childbirth you will suffer great agony and hate it.

And he told the man: you will have to work for your living, labour with the sweat of your brow, and hate that too.

He threw them out the garden. Threw them out of the beautiful garden he had laboured so hard to create.

And then he posted a particularly malevolent and officious being at the entrance to the garden armed with a flaming and particularly sharp sword.

For he didn't want them coming back to the garden, and didn't want them eating the tree of life. He'd wanted them to stay ignorant; and if he couldn't have that, at least he could make sure they both died.

For he wasn't all wise, and he wasn't all powerful. He was frightened.

And he left behind him the division of labour

and an infinity of unhappiness

and was never seen again.

Adam and Eve, weeping bitterly, turned their backs on paradise and never returned.

As we have never returned.

And I'm left trying to remember,

trying to remember as we all must,

all must try to remember

when it was I first ate of that fruit

when was it

I must remember, we all must remember

sometime

otherwise this vague deep down feeling of somehow always being in the wrong

of always being in the wrong somehow and things never ever going to be right

if we don't remember that feeling will never leave us

and things never will be right. Never will be right at all.

It wasn't when I went to school wearing my mother's knickers

because that didn't feel wrong, that just felt peculiar

it wasn't the primary school play when they asked us what did we want to be, gnomes or flowers

and I said 'a flower please'

and was very surprised to see I was the only boy

and it wasn't in the battles in the school playgrounds when the boys were warriors and the girls were nurses who looked after the wounded

and I always got myself wounded early on because I knew I would rather be one of the nurses

and that just seemed sensible

it wasn't even when I was a wolf cub and detested my woggle

because that just felt like a kind of blank.

It was later, when my voice should have been breaking

only it didn't and I felt ashamed to be heard speaking

about then I discovered I was an abomination.

I discovered that God loathed me

that I was an offence in his nostrils

I discovered God despised me

and that the world would despise me too

would despise me and reject me and loathe me and detest me

if ever the world discovered who I really was.

And I don't know, ladies and gentlemen,

ladies and gentlemen and something in between

I don't know if you've ever had the experience

ever had the experience of being an abomination.

I expect you have.

According to the book, you're an abomination if you shave your face.

You're an abomination if you wear clothes that mix fabrics.

And you're also an abomination if you do something with a goat.
Something so terribly technical I'm not even going to begin to explain it.

Being an abomination.

You just live with it, don't you?

And it's not that bad.

I tell you it's better to be mocked

it's better to be laughed at and spat upon

for being whoever you are

better than being a nothing

better than being a blank

better than being someone who cannot be who they truly are.

Where was I?

I was with Adam and Eve, weeping as they left behind the garden

I was with Jehovah thundering on the desert plain

thundering at the Israelites at the foot of the mountain

hurling abuse at me in his book of Leviticus

Hurling abuse at me because he was terrified.

As I was terrified too.

Waging a war on the Mother Goddess

And on her priests who wear drag and look simply gorgeous

Struggling with the Goddess. Struggling with our other half.

Hunting her with nets, piercing her with sharp spears, setting traps for her in dark places and hacking her to pieces with knives.

Mining, gouging, poisoning: making war on our mother. Making war on our mother the earth.

Later we learnt stronger weapons still. Me and God.

Last of all and all the time: oblivion and silence.

Did you know God's name is female?

Elohim. It's feminine plural.

And how hard he's had to work to make us all forget.

And all the male theologians do their best to help him get over his embarrassment by saying that although feminine and plural in form his name is masculine and singular in intention.

God is like a middle-aged man with a wardrobe full of frocks. A closet he keeps firmly locked because he dare not open the door.

And Adam is labouring in a field

And Eve is screaming in the agony of childbirth

And Adam would really like to help but hasn't a notion of what to do.

And look I'm still there. Still listening to these stories, these stories being told me by the man in the white frock, the white frock which isn't a frock, really, but a vestment, and I'm not a wolf cub any more,

I'm older now, I hate my body

I hate my body and I live in my head

I live in my head and I'm trying really hard to be normal.

I'm working really hard to get a scholarship but I keep getting distracted

I keep getting distracted by this yellow dress in a shop window

This yellow dress I would so love to wear

And I know I shouldn't even look at it but I can't stop myself

I can't stop myself and I feel so ashamed.

It's amazing how many yellow dresses there are in the world

How many yellow dresses when you're forbidden to wear them

And yellow dresses and pink dresses and red dresses and blue

And I'm trying to pass my law exams

I'm trying to wear y fronts and be happy!

And I'm dreaming of the day when I'm qualified

When I can put the letters QC after my name

And then I won't be William any more

I'll be Billie Smith QC

Counsel to Queens

And I'll be entitled to wear my wig and gown.

I'll put God in the dock and I'll tell him

I'm conducting a judicial inquiry

that may lead to a criminal prosecution

an inquiry into the nature of God and the story of the book of Genesis.

And I have to warn you God anything you say may be taken down

and used in evidence against you

And God won't dare say a word

Because I shall be so dead scary

And I can cite myself as a witness

and there I'll be in the witness box, about 10 years old,

And I'll wear the yellow frock

this yellow frock, with the flowers on it

And I'll wear the yellow frock and I'll try not to be ashamed.

Observe, I'll say, in my grown-up self,

Ladies and gentlemen of the jury, ladies and gentlemen and something in between. Observe this boy.

For he knows what is right and what is wrong.

He knows in the uncorrupted part of his self that the God of this story was unjust and vindictive

But what they keep telling him, the men in the frocks they claim are not frocks, but are vestments, allegedly, the accomplices in this vile crime, is that the God of this story was supremely just and wise

And so the first lesson he has learnt was not to trust his own perceptions. And we have all learnt it, ladies and gentlemen of the jury and whoever is between: we havc all been corrupted.

But that is only the beginning, ladies and gentlemen of the jury and everything in between, that is only the beginning of the wickedness

Observe the boy

He knows the story is unjust and unfair and so the second lesson he has been taught is that injustice is woven into the very fabric of the world.

That injustice is part of the natural order of things

and that there is nothing anyone can ever do to change it.

But even that is still only the beginning, ladies and gentlemen of the jury and everything in between, that is still only the beginning of God's wickedness.

For the third lesson taught to this innocent boy is that the division into genders is something fundamental,

fixed and immutable,

and that there is shame and there is guilt attached to it.

And worse still:

For the fourth lesson is that the female is inferior to the male and must be subjugated

because she is somehow responsible for all the evil in the world

And so this story,

ladies and gentlemen and everything in between

this story we are taught is one of the most ancient stories we possess

this story we are taught is fundamental,

one of the first and best attempts to understand our world

and give it shape and meaning

this story we are taught is one of the most profound

and sacred texts we shall ever know or read

this story is full of lies

and does us the most profound harm

This boy, this innocent boy in the beautiful yellow dress

has already stopped feeling his body as part of the beautiful world.

This boy feels instead as something separate and tainted

And this is all, ladies and gentlemen of the jury, all the work of this vile book.

This vile book that teaches its victims

that women are inferior and dangerous, and to want to be one is utterly disgusting.

Look at what has happened to this boy

He doesn't know now when it was he first ate the apple

He can't remember when he first opened his eyes

when he looked in the mirror

and detested what he saw there

Detested what he saw because he saw a man,

or a boy turning into a man

and didn't want to be a man.

Didn't want to be a man at all.

So what did he do, ladies and gentlemen of the jury, ladies and gentlemen and something in between?

He did the same as the God in the wicked story.

He did the same as every young boy and every young man who has been exposed to it

every young boy and every young man who thought he didn't measure up

and who was made to be ashamed of his own tears

He split himself in two.

He took out his rib

The part of him closest to his heart,

And he tried to cauterise it, cauterise his own heart

And make it numb.

He took out his rib and he split himself in two.

And became divided into male and female

And the female half he tried to lock up inside himself and trample and forget.

But he could not forget, ladies and gentlemen and something in between, he could never forget.

Because none of us can. None of us ever can.

And as for the boy,

There was the man his body was, and hated,

and there was the woman he thought he really wanted to be.

He hated the man for being manly

and he hated the woman for making him feel ashamed.

And now see him, ladies, gentlemen, something in between:

see him now:

And I grow older and spottier and developed the most shockingly awkward stoop

See the effects of pornography, I'll say,

Watching myself, watching myself declining

Sixteen years old and wearing the vilest male clothes

Sixteen years old and desperate to conform

and never wearing feminine clothes

Except in my dreams

The dreams I try so hard to forget.

But it's useless, his desires are just getting stronger

compulsive and twisted and bitter

He feels perverted and monstrous and utterly alone

But let me point out to you this witness box that has grown quite incredibly large,

No one knows how many victims there are

for they are countless

And we're not just talking here of unhappy boys

But girls and women denied their rights to be fully themselves

Girls and women beaten and tormented by the men in their lives

Because they represent something or someone the man is trying to forget

The man trying to suppress and forget the woman inside

Trying to suppress and forget the woman inside him.

And just how many men are there out there,

Out there in this tormented world
How many men beating their wives?
How many men
Hiding their secret selves
As if they were criminals
Hiding their secret selves or else lamenting their loss
The loss of all their dreams
How many men spending their days in suits
pretending to be normal men
and their nights in dresses
pretending to be normal women
how many hiding feminine selves
in closets, lock-up garages or garden sheds
post office boxes or safe addresses
suitcases hidden under beds
or anonymous packages at the back of chests of drawers
how many closets, would you say,
how many secret cross-dressed places?
How many others out on the streets
taking endless precautions
not to be read not to be noticed
not to be observed.
How many breast implants
how much vocal retraining

how many having testicles removed with pincers

how many having penises cut off with sharp knives

And how many still imprisoned in deep anxiety

of their secret being revealed, of their being discovered

to have committed the so-called crime

of wanting to be female?

And how many men afraid of their tenderness

How many men afraid of being hurt

How many men in the cockpits of fighter planes

the fighter planes circling slowly above our heads?

And look, all of you, look at the witness box overflowing with unhappiness

And this, I will say, me Billie Smith in my wig and gown

Billie Smith, counsel to queens,

all this shocking damage

is only a tiny fraction of the shame and anger and guilt that's been caused by the infinite pornographer going under the name of God.

For this book, this so-called holy book, is pornography. Prima facie. Pornography.

And I base my case, ladies and gentlemen and everybody in between,

I base my case on the classic definition as established in *Regina* vs. *Hicklin* (1868):

Not the common and incorrect definition of being a text picture or moving image that incites us to lust, but in the wider, deeper, truer sense that it demeans and it degrades.

It degrades our capacity to think, degrades our capacity to judge, degrades our sense of what is right.

Above all, it corrupts and degrades those whose minds are open to such immoral influences.

As yours are ladies and gentlemen of the jury

ladies and gentlemen and in betweens

and as was this boy

this boy in the beautiful yellow dress

the beautiful yellow dress he will now wear with pride

And of course I'll win my case

And God will run away from the courtroom

and before anyone knows what's happening

all the bishops'll go to sewing classes

and make real frocks out of all their gorgeous vestments

and they'll allow all the priests to enjoy them

churches will become temples of sexual delight

and the mullahs will be laughing as they fill their beards with flowers

and all the stealth bombers turn into gorgeous butterflies

Where was I?

With Adam. With Adam and Eve.

And Eve left Adam and ran away with Lilith her new best friend

And so there's Adam

poor Adam all lonely

and he's built himself a bunker

a bunker where he lives alone, with God on his side,
a castle-cum-locker room
club house and gentleman's convenience,
built of damp concrete with graffiti on the walls
a decaying fortress where he sulks in aggressive self-pity
without his role as bread winner and useless in the home
Adam and Jehovah, in there together, smelly feet, huge beer bellies,
no good at cooking, useless at cleaning,
with the football on the telly, yelling insults at the ref
lashing out at poofs and at women,
at war with his self, at war with the world

And the young men, the young men in their cockpits
for whom we are just blips on a computer
and flesh and blood
feeling and tenderness
compassion and love
just blips
blips on the computer screen.

The young men, the young men in the fighter planes
circling above our heads
circling closer now
circling ever closer
But look. Look there in the corner

there in the corner of God's bunker
in a tiny corner is a tiny door
And he would love to open it, but he's too afraid

oh go on God open the door
open the door God take a peek inside
it won't kill you.

open the door God open it wide

see its allright really there's a tweed jacket in there
and the most gorgeous green silk sequinned frock
and they're both yours
both yours for the taking
and there's stilettos and walking boots and terribly sensible shoes
open the door God
open the door Adam
open the door heroines
heroines and heroes of this story
God bless the child
Bless the child who has her own
Bless the timid and the shy
For they shall be shameless
Bless the lonely and misunderstood
For she shall have everyone she wants.

Bless the poor. For she shall be rich.

Bless the chairman of the board.

For she shall lose everything!

Bless the boy in the closet in the silk wedding gown For he shall come out

Bless the prostitute

For she shall be honoured

Bless the frigid and the impotent

For they shall have sex for ever and ever!

Amen! Amen!

And bless the fathers who don't care because they've never been cared for

For they shall be loved

Bless the mothers who hit

Because they cannot still their children's tears

For they shall be comforted

Bless the bully and the criminal

For they shall lose all fear

Bless the inadequates who go into government

For they shall lose their power

Bless the gangster who boasts of the women he's raped and victims he's robbed and the enemies he's killed

For he is them

And they are him

And shall be for ever and ever.

Amen amen.

And bless this boy who's been frozen in terror

Remind him he is not alone

Don't let him ever forget

and don't let us, don't let us ever forget

for he is she

and she is he

and we are they

and they are we

and ever shall be

for ever and for ever and for ever

END

Index